Vorwort

Mit dem neuen, spannenden Compact Lernkrimi History können Sie Ihre Englischkenntnisse auf schnelle und einfache Weise vertiefen, auffrischen und überprüfen.
Fesselnde Ereignisse im England vergangener Zeiten machen das Sprachtraining zu einem aufregenden und abwechslungsreichen Erlebnis.
Der Krimi wird auf jeder Seite durch vielfältige und kurzweilige Übungen ergänzt, die das Lernen unterhaltsam und spannend machen.
Prüfen Sie Ihr Englisch in Lückentexten, Zuordnungs- und Übersetzungsaufgaben, in Buchstabenspielen und Kreuzworträtseln!
Ob im Bus oder in der Bahn, im Wartezimmer, zu Hause oder in der Mittagspause – das Sprachtraining im handlichen Format bietet die ideale Trainingsmöglichkeit für zwischendurch.
Schreiben Sie die Lösungen einfach ins Buch!
Die richtigen Antworten sind in einem eigenen Lösungsteil zusammengefasst.

Und nun kann die Spannung beginnen .

Viel Spaß und Erfolg!

Die Ereignisse und die handelnden Personen in diesem Buch sind frei erfunden. Etwaige Ähnlichkeiten mit tatsächlichen Ereignissen und historischen oder lebenden Personen wären rein zufällig und unbeabsichtigt.

Inhalt

Story

England, 14. Jahrhundert: Die Stadt London entwickelt sich zu einer interessanten – aber auch gefährlichen – Metropole.
Innerhalb kurzer Zeit bringt man bereits die zweite Leiche zu Constable Warwicke. Bei beiden Toten wurde der kleine Finger abgetrennt, genauso wie bei einer dritten Leiche … Geht in London ein Serienmörder um?
Bisher hat der Constable noch keinen Verdächtigen. Ist er mit dem ungewöhnlichen Fall überfordert?
Als auch eine gute Freundin des Gentleman John Hathaway dem Mörder zum Opfer fällt, beginnen er und seine kluge Frau Anna auf eigene Faust zu ermitteln. Die Hinweise führen sie nach Canterbury, wo sie einem gut gehüteten Familiengeheimnis auf die Spur kommen. Wird es ihnen gelingen, das Geheimnis zu lüften und den Täter zu stellen, bevor es einen weiteren Toten gibt?

Chapter 1: Another Grim Discovery

The wagon made its way slowly through the streets of London in May 1312. Some streets were broad while others were so narrow that they were only single lanes, but all were dirty and the air was disgusting. The smells of tanners boiling skins and waste thrown directly onto the street overpowered the fresh air which blew in from the countryside. Houses along the street were half-timbered and many had straw roofs which meant the threat of fire was ever-present. The wagon rattled and creaked and added to the many noises of the crowded city. The single horse which pulled it was old and tired. Next to the horse walked a balding, heavy man who held the horse's reins and chased flies away from its eyes with his hat. "Come on, Bess," he said to the horse. Something in the small wagon was covered up. It occasionally moved with the wagon but made no sound. "Come on, Bess," he repeated. "We have to turn here. We're almost there. There's a good old fellow, just keep a move on."

Übung 1: Setzen Sie die Verben der Sätze ins Simple Past!

1. People throw their waste onto the streets.

____

2. Most of the streets are small and narrow.

____

3. The man is holding the horse by the reins.

____

4. They keep moving through the streets.

____

5. A fresh wind is blowing from the countryside.

____

"What did he die of?" a passer-by asked. "It wasn't something you could catch, I hope?"
"He didn't die of the finger that's gone," the driver answered.
"He's missing a finger?" returned the first.
"Aye. But where he's gone to he won't be needing it."
The driver continued until he came to a constable's house. There he stopped and knocked. A moment later, a man in his late-thirties with a goatee answered.
"Good morning, William," the man said.
"Good morning, Constable Warwicke," said the other.
"What brings you here?"
William nodded towards the wagon.
"What do you have there?"
"A body."
"That would have been my first guess. Does the body have a name?" The constable lifted one corner of the cover and saw a pair of black shoes.

ÜBUNG 2 !

Übung 2: Formulieren Sie die passenden Fragen zu den Antworten! Beginnen Sie die Fragen jeweils mit den Fragewörtern in Klammern!

1. He died of a heart attack.

(What) ____

2. He went to the constable's house.

(Where) ____________________

3. He was looking at the man.

(Who) ____________________

4. He spoke of the dead body.

(What) ____________________

5. I have come to talk to you.

(What) ____________________

"It did. Geoffrey de Kronung."
"What was the cause of death?" he asked, as he stepped around the wagon.
"Judging by the marks on the neck…" William began and then his voice faded away.
Constable Warwicke lifted the dirty cover and saw the face of a young man, eyes staring into eternity. "Definitely looks strangled," he said, while examining the bruises on the neck. "Why didn't you close his eyes?"
"I wanted to leave him as he was, sir."
"Then you should have left him where he was. Was he robbed?"
"No, sir. I turned out his pockets, and he still had money."
"Does anything seem to be missing?"
"A finger was cut off."
Constable Warwicke glanced down at the right hand and saw the space for the little finger. This was the second person found murdered and missing the little finger on the right hand.

ÜBUNG 3 !

Übung 3: Korrigieren Sie die Fehler!

1. The horse who pulled the wagon was old and tired.

___

2. The man is missing of a finger.

___

3. Does the horse has a name?

___

4. He left the man how he was.

___

5. Is something missing?

___

6. The constable was lucky that he didn't fell.

___

7. He should left him where he found him.

___

"Was there anyone around who saw anything?"
"No one saw anything."
"As usual. No one ever sees anything, even if something happens out in the open in the crowded street. They don't see a thing. I think half of the inhabitants of this city are blind. Where did you find him?"
"He was just outside the city walls at an inn with a Lion on the sign."

"Why did you bring him to me?"
"Because you asked me to."
"Yes, you are right, now take the body away. Have the family been alerted?"
"Yes. They know he's on the way."
"Don't delay any longer. Take him to the family with our condolences."
With a nod, William turned away and walked up to the horse. "Okay Bess," he said, and gently pulling on the reins began to lead the horse away.
Constable Warwicke watched the wagon move on down the street in the direction of the Thames, then looked at the pile of droppings left behind by the horse and shook his head.

Übung 4: ***Some*** *oder* ***any,*** ***anything*** *oder* ***something,*** ***anybody*** *oder* ***somebody****? Markieren Sie mit richtig ✓ oder falsch – !*

ÜBUNG 4 !

1. Did you see something? ☐
2. The constable asked anything. ☐
3. The inhabitants of the city didn't know something. ☐
4. The man didn't talk to somebody. ☐
5. Did they say anything interesting? ☐
6. There was something missing. ☐
7. Do you have any clue? ☐
8. Does anybody have a question? ☐
9. Do you have some good news? ☐

Mr John Hathaway, Gentleman, happened to be walking by on the pavement when he noticed Constable Warwicke standing and watching a wagon turn the corner.

"Good morning, Constable Warwicke," Mr Hathaway called out. Mr Hathaway was a well-to-do man of the lower nobility, who filled an unpaid position in city government. He was 35 years of age. As soon as the constable saw Mr Hathaway, his face gave way to an almost pleasant smile. "Good morning, Mr Hathaway," he responded. The two men had met some three years earlier when Constable Warwicke had been instrumental in breaking up a group of thieves who had been terrorizing some of the richer residents of London. Constable Warwicke's courage had then been noted even by the Lord Mayor of London.

ÜBUNG 5

Übung 5: Bilden Sie die erste Steigerungsform (Komparativ) des Adjektivs!

1. good ____________
2. early ____________
3. expensive ____________
4. dirty ____________
5. gentle ____________
6. pleasant ____________
7. rich ____________
8. sad ____________
9. big ____________
10. many ____________

"Any news this morning, Constable?" Mr Hathaway asked. "The cart that just left your door seemed to be bearing bad news."
"It was indeed," Constable Warwicke said. "The wagon was carrying the corpse of what was once a young man of moderate means."
"His death was not a natural one?"
"It was murder," Constable Warwicke confirmed.
"How was he murdered?"
"He was strangled."
"Who was it?"
"Geoffrey de Kronung."
"That name seems familiar to me." He thought a moment and then asked, "Are there any other details?"

Übung 6: Lesen Sie weiter und unterstreichen Sie die richtige Zeitform!

Constable Warwicke (1.) looked/has looked up uncomfortably. "What do you mean by 'other details'?"
"I mean", said Mr Hathaway, "something that (2.) made/makes this murder different from others."
Looking even more uncomfortable, he answered, "Indeed there is Mr Hathaway. The young man (3.) is/was not robbed, in the normal way: he was not missing any money, apparently, but only the little finger on his right hand."
"Interesting," Mr Hathaway (4.) said/says.
"What (5.) is/was even more interesting", Constable Warwicke continued, "is that this is not the first corpse to come to me with the little finger of the right hand missing."
"It isn't?" said Mr Hathaway with some surprise. "How many (6.) did/have you had?"
"This one (7.) makes/made two in the space of a fortnight."

"Little fingers", continued Mr Hathaway, "are a strange thing to collect. Many years ago, some crusaders returned with tales of armies of the uncivilized collecting the heads of slain warriors and knights. But why did the man bring the wagon to you?"
"Because I asked him to."
The noise on the street was increasing as the morning progressed, with more people and more traffic on the street, so the two men could no longer comfortably speak. Mr Hathaway therefore wished the constable a good morning and went on his way.
That evening, over a mug of wine, Mr Hathaway told his wife and several friends about the murder.
"And both were missing the same little finger?" asked Mrs Anna Hathaway. She was a lively, fine looking woman of 28 with natural intelligence and curiosity. In the fashion of the day, her long black hair was covered by a white cloth headdress.

ÜBUNG 7 !

Übung 7: Adjektiv oder Adverb? Setzen Sie die Wörter in Klammern in die passende Form!

1. This murder was (different) ____________________ from others.
2. The constable looked up ____________________ (uncomfortable).
3. Mr Hathaway listened ____________________ (attentive).
4. Mr Hathaway (obvious) ____________________ loved his wife Anna.
5. Her black hair was ____________________ (beautiful).
6. The armies of the uncivilized fought ____________________ (cruel).

"But of course," answered another gentleman, older, with a grey beard. "Look at my fingers," he said extending his hands with the

little fingers pointed up. “See how the little finger curves ever so slightly? This is a murderer who notices fine details. He would not go collecting a right finger here and a left finger there.”
“Well”, said the older gentleman’s wife, “I hope he doesn’t take a fancy to your finger.”
“Were both of the victims of the, er, better sort?”
“Honestly”, answered Mr Hathaway, “I didn’t think to ask.”
“That’s just the sort of information you must ask,” the man argued.
“My husband, I’m afraid, is not always a man of details,” Mrs Hathaway protested with a laugh. “He’s better at organising.”
Mr Hathaway, being a good-natured man, only smiled in answer. He knew that the wife of his friend would never have dreamed of making such a criticism of her husband.
“The young man’s name was Geoffrey de Kronung,” Mr Hathaway reported.
“I know that name, de Kronung,” said the bearded man.
“I know it, too”, Mrs Hathaway said, “but from where?”
“Now who lacks the details?” Mr Hathaway asked, triumphantly.

Übung 8: Lesen Sie weiter und setzen Sie die richtigen Präpositionen ein!
(at (2x), of (2x), on, in (2x), from)

Constable Warwicke was sitting (1.) __________ a tavern, the Five Arrows, which were carved (2.) __________ the sign outside the pub, with a pint of ale. Next to him sat Henry de Luce, another (3.) __________ London’s constables. The two men rarely looked (4.) __________ each other. Instead, they stared (5.) __________ the others in the pub. In the light thrown by the candles hanging (6.) _________ the ceiling in a few places, they could not see everyone. Constable Warwicke had just been telling of his day, concluding with what had actually come first – the body missing the little finger of the right hand.

"And you say this was the second one?" asked Constable de Luce, after taking a sip (7.) _________ his ale and then wiping his mouth on his shirt sleeve.

"The second one (8.) _________ a fortnight."

"So he will strike again and again until he is captured."
"He will not strike again and again," Constable Warwicke declared. "I will have him and very soon, indeed."
"Do you know who it is already?"
"No, no, I don't", Constable Warwicke admitted, "but I have a talent for finding my men, as you well know," he added arrogantly. Ever since he had been recognized by the Lord Mayor, friends and colleagues had noticed a significant change in him. He was more confident and seldom took advice. It was true, however, that he had displayed a singular talent for difficult cases.

ÜBUNG 9 !

Übung 9: Infinitiv oder Verlaufsform? Setzen Sie das Verb in Klammern in die richtige Form!

1. (be) _______________ recognized by the Lord Mayor, Constable Warwicke had changed significantly.

2. Hathaway didn't have a talent for (recognize) ________________ details.

3. Constable Warwicke was confident about (find) ________________ the murderer.

4. He didn't (think of) ________________ the danger.

5. Warwicke was about (leave) ________________.

"Well, Warwicke, where do you begin?"
"Both bodies were found right outside the city walls, so I will be going out there a bit more often."
"They were found out in the countryside?"
"No. The one from this morning was found in an inn, just outside the walls. The other was along the Fleet River, not far from where it meets the Thames."
"If you need help, you can always send for me."
"I won't need any help, thank you very much," Constable Warwicke declared and took a long swallow of his ale.
"But, if you ever do…"
Constable Warwicke laughed a moment. "Thank you, Luce, but I will manage quite well by myself."

Chapter 2: Meetings in Inns and Elsewhere

Mr Hathaway found himself in the inn at the sign of the Five Arrows. He was not a regular at the inn, which was frequented by all kinds of people but only a few noblemen like himself.

Übung 10: Unterstreichen Sie alle Verben im Simple Past!

Mr Hathaway was on his way home from his position in city government. Amongst other things, his job involved maintaining lists of incoming and outgoing ships, their home port or destination and their purpose in travelling, for example their cargo.

"Good day, Mr BonHomme," said Mr Hathaway to a well-dressed young man of about his standing.

"Good day, Mr Hathaway," answered this young man.

"Is there anything new?" asked Mr Hathaway.

Mr BonHomme worked in city administration, as well, dealing with the problem of providing safe water to the city of London. Water was a problem that was proving to be more challenging than he and others in the administration could deal with.

"The news? I heard that there has been another murder. A young man was found dead and missing a finger."

"Missing a finger?" asked Mr Hathaway. "That makes three now."

"I heard it was two," Mr BonHomme answered.

"The second was found just two weeks ago," answered Mr Hathaway. "Do you know the name of the third person who was found murdered?"

"It was a de Bruyere, that's all I know," responded the other.

"That cannot be." Mr Hathaway looked around the inn for a moment and then saw Constable Warwicke in his accustomed corner, sitting next to another constable.

"Let's go over and speak with Constable Warwicke a moment and get the whole story. He will certainly know it."

Mr BonHomme looked as if he did not like the idea of going over to speak with the constable. The flickering light cast dark shadows across Constable Warwicke's face, making him appear to be a disagreeable person.

"I know him," Mr Hathaway added. "I worked with him several years ago. He is a talented constable, courageous too. The Lord Mayor even recognized him for bravery."

Übung 11: Übersetzen Sie!

1. Viele verschiedene Menschen besuchten die Schenke.

2. Jeden Tag saß Constable Warwicke an seinem Stammplatz.

3. Es war schwierig, die Londoner Innenstadt mit reinem Wasser zu versorgen.

4. Dieses Problem stellte sich als Herausforderung dar.

5. Mr Hathaway wollte mit Constable Warwicke sprechen.

Mr Hathaway led Mr BonHomme over to the constable.
"Constable Warwicke," said Mr Hathaway. "I hope I am not disturbing you?"
"No, not at all, Mr Hathaway," the constable responded, though it appeared to be quite likely that he was simply being polite.
"Mr BonHomme, this is Constable Warwicke. Constable Warwicke, Mr BonHomme."

"Pleasure to meet you," said the constable and then introduced the man sitting next to him, Constable Henry de Luce.
"Is it true", asked Mr Hathaway, "that another body has been found without a finger?"
"Yes, it's true," Constable Warwicke acknowledged.
"What is the name of the victim this time?"
"James de Bruyere."
"James de Bruyere? I know Robert de Bruyere," Mr Hathaway said, concerned.
"They might be related," Constable Warwicke suggested.
"Where was the body found?" Mr Hathaway continued.
"In St Mary Magdalene Church."
"In a church?" asked Mr BonHomme.
"Aye," said the constable.

! ÜBUNG 12

*Übung 12: Ersetzen Sie **might** mit der passenden Form von **be allowed to** oder **it is possible that**!*

1. Might I ask the name of the victim?

____

2. They might not talk about the murdered man.

____

3. Might we come in?

____

4. Robert de Bruyere and James de Bruyere might be related.

____

5. She might be right.

"What are you doing to capture the murderer?" Mr BonHomme asked. "Who has been given the task of finding his murderer?" "Take my word on this," said Constable Warwicke visibly angry. "I have everything under control. I have no need of sergeants or clerks. I will settle this myself."
"But the murderer has struck again," Constable de Luce argued. "I don't see how you can say you have everything under control."
"I said to take my word, Luce," Constable Warwicke said and slammed his mug down on the table. Ale flew all over the table and some splashed onto the two gentlemen standing across from the two constables. Constable Warwicke stood and stormed out of the inn.
"He is a most impolite fellow, Hathaway," said Mr BonHomme.
"He's a man of character," Mr Hathaway responded. "You cannot judge him as you would judge others."

Übung 13: Ersetzen Sie in den folgenden Sätzen die of-Konstruktion durch den s-Genitiv!

1. The wife of Mr Hathaway was beautiful.

---

2. Mr BonHomme ignored the words of the constable.

---

3. The name of the last victim was de Bruyere.

---

4. The ale of Constable Warwicke flew all over the table.

____

5. Mr Hathaway explained the behaviour of Warwicke.

____

6. Constable de Luce was a friend of Warwicke.

____

Mr BonHomme made a face to show that he did not quite agree. "Does he have help?" Mr Hathaway asked Constable de Luce.
"I have offered him my help several times", Constable de Luce answered, "but he has rejected me each time." It was clear to Mr Hathaway that Constable de Luce viewed his friend with a mixture of admiration and dislike. "He thinks he needs no help."
"I can see that," Mr BonHomme agreed. "He thinks he has no equals."
"At least no equals amongst the constables," Constable de Luce returned. "He doesn't pretend to be at your rank."
"Thank you," Mr Hathaway said to Constable de Luce. "You are a real friend to Constable Warwicke, even if he does not see that himself."
The two men then left Constable de Luce and walked back to another part of the inn where they ordered two more ales.

ÜBUNG 14 !

*Übung 14: Setzen Sie **him, her, himself, herself** oder **the** ein!*

1. He found ___________ at the Five Arrows Inn.

2. Mr Hathaway loved his wife and respected ___________.

3. Constable Warwicke wasn't able to control __________.

4. She could speak for __________.

5. Mr BonHomme judged __________ as he judged others.

6. She was __________ one who always knew what __________ husband was thinking.

7. Warwicke's behaviour didn't seem unusual to __________.

8. The constable wanted to find the murderer __________.

"Just to calm the nerves after meeting your volatile friend," said Mr BonHomme, lifting his mug.

Mr Hathaway lifted his mug as well.

"So you know someone related to the murdered person?" Mr BonHomme asked.

"I do," Mr Hathaway answered. "I think we should finish our drink and make a journey to Robert de Bruyere. He is a friend and I should like to offer my sympathies if this James de Bruyere is a brother I am unfamiliar with."

The two men finished their drinks and then entered the dark streets of London. In the early evening there were fewer people on the street than there had been at midday. A half-moon in the sky provided the streets with some light. On nights when there was no moon, the streets were often more dangerous than usual. People walked along in groups of two or more, usually. The two men walked to an area close to the Strand, where only the very rich lived. Neither Mr Robert de Bruyere, Mr Hathaway nor Mr BonHomme lived on the Strand but they did not live far away. They walked up to a fairly large house and Mr Hathaway knocked. A manservant answered the door.

Übung 15: Lesen Sie weiter und unterstreichen Sie alle Adjektive im folgenden Textabschnitt!

"Is Mr Robert de Bruyere at home?"
"He is. Please come in."
The two men walked into a small foyer.
"May I tell him who is calling?"
"Mr John Hathaway and Mr Harold BonHomme."
In a minute, the manservant returned and brought them upstairs to a sitting room which was quite dark, being only half-lit by candles.
"Good evening, gentlemen," said a man of 25, with light brown hair and deep pock marks on his cheeks. This was Mr Robert de Bruyere. "Good evening, Hathaway."
After introductions and the usual formalities, Mr Hathaway said, "I wanted to speak to you about something that might be of importance to you."
"Yes, what is it?"
"I heard about the death of James de Bruyere and I was wondering if that might be your brother."
"I thought that might be the reason for your visit. No, he is not my brother," he said, with sadness still in his voice. "I do have two brothers", he said to Mr BonHomme, "Harold and Andrew, as well as a sister, Mary. James de Bruyere is our cousin."
"We offer our deepest sympathy for your loss," Mr BonHomme said with great formality.

"It is sad that someone so young – he was only 21 years old – should die," Mr de Bruyere admitted. "And then to die in a church, a place of holiness and peace. The Good Lord must have turned away for a second when the murderer entered. He could hardly believe that such an action would take place there."

"Be careful what you say," said a female voice.
The two visitors now turned their attention to the darkness behind Mr de Bruyere. There sat two women, one in her early twenties and the one who had spoken, in her early forties.
"This", said Mr de Bruyere, "is my mother, Mrs Clotilde de Bruyere and this is my wife Mrs Laura de Bruyere."
"We are sorry to hear of your loss," Mr Hathaway said.
"It is especially hard for my husband," said Mrs Clotilde de Bruyere. "James was the eldest son of his brother. My husband was, moreover, the Godfather of the unfortunate young man."
"God will one day punish the murderer," said Mr BonHomme.
"I'm sure. But I hope that he is stopped before he murders any others. He must be stopped and soon."

! ÜBUNG 16

Übung 16: Bilden Sie die passenden Substantive zu den Adjektiven und enträtseln Sie das Lösungswort!

1. active _ ☐ _ _ _ _
2. light ☐ _ _ _ _
3. lose _ ☐ _ _
4. deep _ _ _ ☐ _
5. female _ _ _ ☐ _ _ _ _ _ _
6. holy _ _ ☐ _ _ _ _ _
7. dangerous ☐ _ _ _ _ _
8. dark _ _ _ _ _ ☐ _ _

Lösung: _ _ _ _ _ _ _ _

"Losing a relation is always difficult," Mr Hathaway agreed.
"It is indeed," Mr de Bruyere said, staring at the hard wood floor. "But losing him this way makes it all the harder. We have to hope there was some reason behind it that we will one day understand."
"I cannot see any reason behind murdering a 21 year old man in a church," the elder Mrs de Bruyere answered.
"I did not say that I could, Mother" said Mr de Bruyere.
Into the room walked Mary FitzPaulding, née de Bruyere. She was in her early twenties and was considered a great beauty, despite the scars on her face from illness. She was dressed in a bright blue and yellow gown.
"I thought I heard a familiar and friendly voice," she said with a brief yet warm smile as she looked at Mr Hathaway.

! ÜBUNG 17

Übung 17: Setzen Sie die Verben in Klammern in die richtige Zeitform!

"I (1. hear) _______________ the bad news and just thought I should come by and (2. offer) _______________ my sympathy.
"Thank you," she (3. answer) _______________, looking down.
"We had better be going," Mr Hathaway announced. "It is getting late and you have had a long, difficult day."
"We have all had a difficult day", Mr de Bruyere (4. agree) _______________, "and when we get tired we sometimes become a bit argumentative. I'll see you out."
The two men (5. say) _______________ good night to the three women and then followed Mr de Bruyere out. At the door, it looked

as if Mr de Bruyere was about (6. speak) _______________ and was then overcome by emotion. "Good night and thank you for coming," he said after a moment.

The two men (7. walk) _______________ out into the dark street again and walked together.

"I hope your Constable Warwicke (8. find) _______________ the killer soon," Mr BonHomme said.

"I hope he (9. do) _______________, too."

"He should not let his pride get in the way of asking for help," Mr BonHomme added.

"You may not know this", Mr Hathaway said, "but he is the one responsible for making the streets in this area safe. Several years ago there was a group of thieves operating around here and he got rid of every one of them."

"He must know what he is doing", Mr BonHomme declared, "but even people who know what they are doing sometimes need help."

"It seems to be a matter of honour for him, however, so it is best if he just completes his tasks without any interference."

Chapter 3: Unpleasant Meetings

For nearly three months no more victims were found with their little fingers hacked off. Life went on as normal in London, with trade and sales, and people being born, living and dying. Nearly every day, it seemed, some person or family entered the city and did not leave, so the population of London was steadily growing. Some walked in barefoot, while others came on horse or in carriages pulled by one, two or four horses. Due to overcrowding, some of the wealthier citizens enjoyed day trips which took them out of the city and into the countryside, where they could rest and relax, enjoying the fresh air. It was just after coming back from such a day that Mr Hathaway learned of her death.

! ÜBUNG 18

Übung 18: Wie lauten die Sätze? Bringen Sie die Wörter in die richtige Reihenfolge!

1. streets duty it Warwicke's make to was the safe

____

2. believed needed Warwicke BonHomme that Mr help

____

3. constable murderer for the it a matter of to find the honour himself was

____

4. the Mr pride Bonhomme constable's criticized

____

5. people to moved becoming London which many was overcrowded

____

In September 1312, the familiar wagon once again made its way towards Constable Warwicke. The heavy-set driver, smelling of sweat and ale, knocked on the door. After a moment, it opened silently and only darkness stared out from within.

"You'll not be wanting to see me today –" William began.
"And you will not be wanting to see me either," came an answer from the door, sounding more like a vicious animal than a man.
"And yet, something which was once –" continued William.
"Shut up, man, if you are a man. Get out of my sight and take that wagon and its decaying contents with you," he screamed so forcefully that the horse immediately began to move without so much as a "Come on, Bess."
The house door slammed and seemed to echo across the street for several moments.
"Slow, Bess, we want to make her last ride a gentle one even if she won't be able to give us a tip. That's right, Bess, she might once have been able to give us a tip and now she could tell us what she's seeing if her tongue wasn't covered with the white powder that did her in."

Übung 19: Ersetzen Sie in den folgenden Sätzen das Hilfsverb ***can*** *mit der entsprechenden Form von* ***be able to*****:**

1. A good constable can find the murderer himself.

____

2. Wealthy people could make daytrips to the countryside.

____

3. There they could rest and relax.

____

4. She could ride a horse quite well.

____

5. Can you give us a tip?

____

6. Can anybody help us find the inn?

____

Standing in Mr Hathaway's living room was a figure that looked none too happy to be there and held a hat covering his heart.
"It is Mary FitzPaulding. She was found poisoned this afternoon, a white powder having been stuffed into her mouth. She was pale, ivory-coloured, almost a bluish ivory. The powder was still in her mouth as she was found. Your friend Robert de Bruyere is out of his mind with grief. He has sworn vengeance on the killer."
Mr Hathaway fell into a chair and looked at the person who had brought such bad news, Mr Harold BonHomme.
"Since we visited Mr Bruyere several months ago, I thought I would bring you the news myself. I knew you had left the city for the day."

ÜBUNG 20 !

Übung 20: Setzen Sie die Verben in Klammern in die entsprechenden Lücken ein!
(missing, spoke, gone, gaining, unfolded, covering, was, returned, kept, were, seeing)

Finally able to speak, Mr Hathaway said, "Thank you, BonHomme. I think I would have preferred to remain ignorant if it would have (1.) ______________ her alive a little longer in my memory. There was a part of her alive in me that is now (2.) ______________. I miss it and I miss her."

"(3.) ______________ there something between you?" Mr Bon-Homme asked quietly, a look of surprise and concern on his face.

"Between us?" Mr Hathaway (4.) ________________, as if he didn't understand the question. He stared at the wooden ceiling crossed by two beams a moment and then (5.) ________________, "We (6.) ______________ not friends the way her brother and I are." He stopped speaking a moment and looked at Mr BonHomme without (7.) ________________ him. "But", he continued, "there was a time when I thought we would be something more to each other. And then events (8.) ________________ differently and now I am happily married to Anna."

"Oh," Mr BonHomme said, (9.) ________________ his mouth with his hand.

"And she is now (10.) ________________ a finger, just like the other three?" Mr Hathaway asked, his voice (11.) ________________ in strength.

"I'm afraid she is."

"Some beast has taken her life and collected her finger as if he were collecting the antlers from a deer or fur from a rabbit."

Mr BonHomme decided to leave. Some men become enraged immediately, while others wake slowly to rage. The second are sometimes more dangerous: although they do not burn as brightly, they also do not burn out as quickly. They burn strong and long.

Mrs Hathaway came to her husband when she heard the door shut.

"What's wrong, John?" she asked. "You look as if you have just lost your best friend."

"I have not lost my best friend, but there's been another murder."

"Another one?"

"Another murder where the little finger has been 'collected'."

"I thought that had stopped. It has been months now." She was silent for a moment. "Who was it this time?"

"This time, Anna, it was Mary FitzPaulding."

ÜBUNG 21 !

Übung 21: Welches Wort ist das „schwarze Schaf"? Unterstreichen Sie das nicht in die Reihe passende Wort!

1. poisoned, met, murdered, killed
2. asked, said, swore, stuffed
3. ago, earlier, after, before
4. quietly, pale, gently, silently
5. become, get, receive, obtain
6. my, your, ours, her

Mrs Hathaway immediately broke into sobs and buried her head in her husband's shirt and coat. Her headdress fell to the floor. When she had recovered, she said, "Poor Robert. He must be miserable."

"I have to go to him now. It's my duty."

"By all means. Let us go immediately," said Mrs Hathaway.

Mr and Mrs Hathaway did go to Robert de Bruyere's house and there they found the family in tears of bitterness. Robert de Bruyere and his brothers were promising vengeance. Mr Hathaway offered what little comfort he could and then they went on their way. It was late night, when the Hathaways got home.

The following day, Mr Hathaway took a carriage to the door of Constable Warwicke's house. He got down and paid the driver. The street was noisy, dirty, and smelly and he was coming to Constable Warwicke wanting some answers.

A knock on the door was answered only with silence. He knocked even more forcefully, repeatedly, until the door finally opened. No one came out, so Mr Hathaway walked in. A thin woman of about 30 or so, a simple headdress set hastily on her hair, was standing just inside the door. She stared at Mr Hathaway silently.

"I would like to speak with Constable Warwicke."

"He is not available at the moment," she said. It was a reply that made it unclear whether the constable was at home or not.

"I would like to see him, anyway. Is he here?"

The woman repeated herself.

"Is he gone? When do you expect him back?"

"Yes, he's gone. He isn't himself," she added in a whisper.

Übung 22: Lesen Sie weiter und unterstreichen Sie die sechs Wörter, die falsch geschrieben sind! Geben Sie die richtige Schreibweise an!

! ÜBUNG 22

Suddenly, there was a sound upstares, the sound of a piece of wood striking the wodden floor angrily.

"Who's that?" Mr Hathaway asked, walking towards the stairs leading to the first floor.

"That's Constabel Warwicke, but he does not want to see anybody at the moment."

"The devil with what he wants," Mr Hathaway said, and without anything further he ran up the stairs. At the top, he came to a door on his left and nocked on it. “Constable Warwicke, this is Mr Hathaway. I want to speak with you imediately.” He knew this was not the way to speak to the constable, but it expressed the intencity of his emotions well.

1. ______________ 2. ______________ 3. ______________

4. ______________ 5.______________ 6. ______________

The sound of several slow steps moving towards the door were easily heard and then the door opened. The face looking back at Mr Hathaway was, indeed, that of Constable Warwicke but somehow different. There was a cut on one cheek, a black eye, and clearly wounds on an arm and a leg now wrapped with rags.
“You look as though you were in a sword fight,” Mr Hathaway said. Constable Warwicke said nothing, just walked away from the door, using a piece of wood to support himself. Mr Hathaway stood in the hall a moment but then followed the constable inside.
“What happened,” Mr Hathaway said.
“It’s one of the dangers of my work,” Constable Warwicke said at last, his voice almost unfriendly. “A well-armed thief comes out at night and strikes before he can be seen.”

ÜBUNG 23 !

Übung 23: Setzen Sie die fehlenden Präpositionen ein!
(in (3x), at, of (2x), on, from)

1. He was looking __________ Mr Hathaway.

2. Constable Warwicke had a wound __________ his arm.

3. He had been involved __________ a fight.

4. Hathaway was walking away __________ his house.

5. He was not invited __________ by the strange woman.

6. __________ 1312 the London population increased.

7. These are the pleasures __________ my work.

8. She was a thin woman __________ 30 years.

There was a silence between the two men. Neither looked at the other. He thinks, Mr Hathaway thought, that I am weak, but he will find out that I can be very difficult if I have to be. I spent years going out into the fields outside London nearly every weekend jousting and fencing. I am like a bear that looks friendly but can be deadly.
"You've heard about Mary FitzPaulding, haven't you?" Mr Hathaway asked, breaking a long silence.
"Aye, I have." A threat seemed to hide behind or within these words.
"We all thought the murderer had disappeared and now he has returned."
Constable Warwicke said nothing.
"I know that, in your condition, you cannot do anything to find the murderer –"
"What do you mean, 'in my condition'?"
"You're wounded, Constable. I have not seen your wounds, but as far as I can tell it is not even certain you will survive them."
"I am, indeed, wounded but I will be better straight away, and I will be after this murderer again."

Übung 24: Geben Sie die zwei Steigerungsformen an!

1. angry __________ __________

2. bad __________ __________

3. friendly ______________ ______________

4. difficult ______________ ______________

5. weak ______________ ______________

6. slow ______________ ______________

"He is back, and I do not think there is anything you can do about it, on your own. This murderer has struck again. He left and now he has come back."

"Is that what happened?" Constable Warwicke asked, sarcastically.

"That is what happened, Constable. Because he killed someone dear to me and I plan on seeing that he does not kill again."

"And just how are you going to stop him? Do you know magic?"

"I planned on offering my services to you, but now –"

"Never mind that. I work alone. I don't need your help and I don't need the help of my sergeants," he said rudely.

"You need help desperately," Mr Hathaway answered.

"Is that how you see it?"

"It is." They looked at each other a moment, their faces very close.

"I do not think you can do this alone," Mr Hathaway said at last.

"You don't think I can do my work?" The constable's voice was suddenly quiet and deadly.

ÜBUNG 25 !

Übung 25: Lesen Sie weiter und übersetzen Sie die vorgegebenen Wörter!

"No," Mr Hathaway (1. antwortete) ______________ immediately and (2. laut) ______________. "I do not think you can do your job. So far you have (3. erlaubt) ______________ four people to die at the hand of one murderer. You are not to blame for the first, but for this one I hold you (4. verantwortlich) _______________. People offered help and you rejected it."

"None of you (5. könnte) __________ help me."

"You are proud and foolish, Constable Warwicke. Constable de Luce (6. angeboten) __________ you aid and you rejected it. A man who puts his own honour before the needs of the community he is sworn to protect does not know the meaning of honour."

"That's an attack on my honour. I will see you on the field with swords."

"You do not challenge me," Mr Hathaway (7. sagte) __________, since he was in the nobility and the constable was not. "What makes you think I would honour you with a duel?"

"I may not be a nobleman, but I have a noble heart," he yelled, pounding himself on the chest. "And I challenge you once again."

"I will gladly fight you, but first, since you cannot do it, I am going to find out who (8. tötete) __________ Mary FitzPaulding."

"Get out of here, before I cut you down right here," Constable Warwicke roared.

"I'll leave once I have the name of the first person (9. ermordet) ____________."

"I'll say nothing further to you," Constable Warwicke said, hate in his voice. "My sword will speak for me next."

"You *will* tell me the name of the first person he murdered or I will make sure you lose your position. If I cannot do it, then the de Bruyeres and their allies can. Someone will make sure you have nothing further to do here and that you leave London in disgrace. Now tell me, who was it?"
Constable Warwicke stared at Mr Hathaway. It was a hard stare such as a snake hunting a frog might give.
Mr Hathaway stared right back at Constable Warwicke.
"You're lucky that I'm master of myself at the moment," the constable said. "The first person murdered was Linus Groenig."
"I do not recognize that name. Was he from London?"
"How could you expect to know the name of every person in a city the size of London?"
"I knew de Bruyere. And the name of the second victim, de Kronung, seemed familiar, too. Now, where was this Linus Groenig from?"
"He wasn't from London, though he was found here at Newgate, near Grey Friars."
"Where was he from?"
After a moment of silence, the constable said, "Canterbury."

ÜBUNG 26 !

Übung 26: Setzen Sie das passende Fragewort ein!

1. ______________ did he come from?

2. ______________ was the name of the first victim?

3. ______________ was the first person murdered?

4. ____________ could I know his name?

5. ____________ did he come home from his trip?

6. ____________ finger was it?

"Canterbury? What was he doing here?"
"I don't know. But if you think you're so clever, you can work it out."
"I will," Mr Hathaway said, getting up to leave.
"I won't forget our appointment on the field of honour."
"Neither will I. I welcome that meeting, Constable."
"I will be healthy soon."
"I hope so, because I want this murderer off the streets of London as soon as possible."

Chapter 4: A Journey to Canterbury

Returning from the funeral for Mary FitzPaulding, both Mr and Mrs Hathaway were sad and quiet. Under gentle candlelight, they drank an herbal infusion and ate a little food.
"The first thing we need to do", said Mrs Hathaway, finally, "is to get as much information as possible about the murders."
"What do you mean by 'we', my dear?" her husband asked.
"'We' means you and me."
"I don't want you involved in such a grim business."
"I know what Mary FitzPaulding meant to you, John. I know you do not want any more people to die and you want Mary's murderer found and punished. I want to help you, and I will help you."
"This is not work for a woman."

ÜBUNG 27

Übung 27: Ist die Pluralbildung in den folgenden Sätzen korrekt? Markieren Sie mit richtig ✔ oder falsch – !

1. We have to obtain a great deal of informations. ☐
2. He made a lot of progresses. ☐
3. She got the latest news. ☐
4. Many peoples lived in London. ☐
5. Two millions pounds is a lot of money. ☐
6. She has read two dozen books. ☐

"Indeed it is not", Mrs Hathaway agreed, "and it is not work for a gentleman such as yourself. But you need my help. I am not like these other women, passive and weak. I am intelligent, and I can take care of myself. I am also a bit more cunning. Besides, I have a practical mind. I am more practical than you are."

"Where do we start then?"

"As I said, we need to get as much information as we can about the murders. We need the location, day, and time of the murders. We need to know more about the people who have been murdered as that might tell us why they were murdered."

ÜBUNG 28

Übung 28: Lesen Sie weiter und ordnen sie die Buchstaben zu einem sinnvollen Wort!

"Maybe it was all (1. ramond) ____________."

"John", said Mrs Hathaway, (2. shikang) ____________ her head, "you do not cut off the little finger of the right hand of your (3. civimt) __________ unless it has some special significance.

I think that we will find there is a (4. atternp) ____________ here, if we only look closely enough."

"He's a madman, Anna."

"Of course he is. A (5. fectrepyl) ____________ normal person does not go around killing and cutting off fingers. But that does not mean, my dear husband, that he is not selective in his (6. oichec) ____________ of victims. There may be a larger story playing out here."

"Anna, you are simply bored and looking for (7. tixetemnec) ____________. This is not the place to find your excitement."

"I am bored," she admitted. "Nobody is honest here. Everything is formality and a great deal of talking without saying anything. This, however, is a chance to make a difference."

"Well", her husband said, after thinking a moment," it may not be dangerous from the beginning, so you can help now. But if or when it becomes dangerous, I will lock you up somewhere safe, so you do not put yourself in danger."

Mrs Hathaway laughed and Mr Hathaway joined in.

"So, first we need the dates, approximate times and the locations of the murders," Mrs Hathaway began. "Then we need the cause of death. One thing is clear with poor Mary's death: the murderer is no longer content to kill men. Today is the Sabbath, so we can do nothing. Tomorrow, my husband, you must get the information."

"Some of it we already know."

"When did James de Bruyere die?"

"Three months ago or more."

"That's not good enough, John. We need exact dates. We need family information on them as well. What standing in society do their various families have? Were they in business with someone who is now murdering them?"

! ÜBUNG 29

Übung 29: Bilden Sie sinnvolle Fragesätze!

1. from from is London Canterbury or he

___

2. business their were they murderer in with

___

3. me you have information for got any

___

4. standing friends what their are

___

5. murdered were where de Bruyere you when was

___

Early the following morning, Mr Hathaway entered one of the city administration buildings. This building was constructed of thick stone rather than the half-timber style of most of London's buildings. It was cool in spring and difficult to heat in winter but it was less at risk of burning down. Mr Hathaway spoke with a clerk about Geoffrey de Kronung. He got a date for the death of Mr de Kronung and found that the young man did not come from London originally but Canterbury, too. He had been a merchant with a successful business, but nothing else was known about his background. His body had been sent back to Canterbury for burial. He then learned that Mr Linus Groenig had been killed by stabbing, just as James de Bruyere, whilst Geoffrey de Kronung had been strangled. In London there was no further information on Groenig, so Mr Hathaway decided that a trip to Canterbury, just over 60 miles away, was unavoidable.

"I have arranged for a carriage. We are off to Canterbury at first light tomorrow morning," Mr Hathaway said to his wife as soon as he saw her, sitting at the wooden table which was loaded down with food.

Übung 30: Welches Wort ist das „schwarze Schaf"?

ÜBUNG 30 !

1. clerk, administration, secretary, assistant
2. merchant, trader, dealer, constable
3. burial, funeral, body, cremation
4. stab, wound, shoot, carry
5. unavoidable, unbelievable, inevitable, fated
6. confused, content, satisfied, happy

"Dress in warm clothing," he added.

"Are we to go alone?"

"No. BonHomme is coming with us."

"Must he?" Mrs Hathaway asked. "Please find another person to accompany us, please."

"I have already asked him to come along, as it is safer with two men plus the driver. Besides, he is good with a sword."

"But he is so boring," Mrs Hathaway complained. "He is formal and stiff, and he says absolutely nothing interesting."

Übung 31: Unterstreichen Sie die englische Entsprechung der folgenden Wörter im Text! ***(schlammig, unpassierbar, Diebe, Koffer, Dolche, gutaussehend, kahl, Erscheinung, ärgerlich)***

The carriage left London early, soon after the sun had risen in the east. It was an open carriage as were all at this time. The journey to Canterbury would take six to eight hours, if all went well – which meant that there was not too much rain which made the paths muddy, or even impassable, and that there were no thieves. They were dressed in warm clothes and each brought a trunk with lighter clothes and clothes for any formal occasions that might take place. They also brought a basket of food along for the journey. Finally, Mr Hathaway and Mr BonHomme brought swords and daggers, in case the need for them should arise.
Mr BonHomme sat opposite the Hathaways. Unfortunately for Mrs Hathaway he sat across from her. She tried to look out at the countryside passing by but was forever looking at him. He was not a very handsome man, she thought. He was not quite 30, and yet the top of his head was bald which added another five years to his appearance. Everything else, his clothing, the way he held his arms crossed, the way he turned his head, seemed to be following some social law exactly, without the least bit of individuality. Naturally, Mrs Hathaway found everything about him annoying.

These long journeys by carriage were boring and uncomfortable. Luckily, theirs would only be a day – at most a day and a half if there were serious troubles with the carriage. Looking out at the countryside, the passing scenery, the trees and fields and hills, would only be interesting for a while. The sun rose up higher and conversation stopped. They each fell asleep only to be awoken by the shaking of the carriage and looked out at the countryside and talked. Mr BonHomme shared Mr Hathaway's idea about the murderer.

Übung 32: Bilden Sie aus den Substantiven die entsprechenden Adjektive!

1. opposition ______________________
2. mud ______________________
3. warmth ______________________
4. youth ______________________
5. creativity ______________________
6. length ______________________
7. interest ______________________

"He is just a madman, nothing more. Who knows why he chose the right little finger and who cares? The fact is, that's how we know it is him. It is his mark."

"Until we know something about the victims, it is impossible to say for certain that he is simply a madman," Mrs Hathaway answered.

"But it is so," Mr BonHomme argued. As evidence he had only his opinion, which did not carry much weight with Mrs Hathaway.

Mrs Hathaway frowned at him but said nothing for the moment. "Well", she said to her husband at last, "it may be that this trip is for nothing. But let us keep our eyes and ears open and ask questions and see what we learn."

"Canterbury", said Mr BonHomme several hours later, "is a miserable town, and I for one hope we do not stay there very long."

"Come, BonHomme," said Mr Hathaway. "It has much fresher air than our London air, for instance."

"The water is cleaner, too," Mrs Hathaway added.

"But there is nothing to do there, and the people are so boring."

"Have you already been there?" Mrs Hathaway asked.
"No, indeed. I have not had that pleasure. It is one of the reasons I decided to accompany you."
"How can you have an opinion about a place you have never seen with your own eyes?" Mrs Hathaway asked, amazed.
"I believe, madame, that it is best to have an opinion on a subject. Whether it is based on experience or intuition does not matter. The main thing is to have an opinion, to have given the matter some thought."

! ÜBUNG 33

Übung 33: Welche der beiden Varianten ist die richtige? Unterstreichen Sie!

"Canterbury is a place, Mr BonHomme", she (1.) responded/asked, "it is not a philosophical issue."
Mrs Hathaway (2.) deliberately/happily looked out at the passing trees and fields and said nothing more for several hours and nothing more to Mr BonHomme than was (3.) immediately/absolutely necessary for politeness. Mr BonHomme, for his part, thought Mrs Hathaway had no business speaking to him in the way she (4.) had/has. Later (5.) at/in the afternoon, while Mr BonHomme (6.) slept/sleeps, Mrs Hathaway asked (7.) after/for the information that Mr Hathaway had collected. She glanced at all the (8.) informations/information, (9.) who/which was not very much, and immediately noticed (10.) something/anything.
"Do you not see that already there is a pattern, John?" she asked her husband.

"No," he answered sharply. "I see nothing, except four people dead and four little fingers missing."

“Look”, she suggested, “at the dates of their deaths.”
”Anna, this is no time to be a teacher. Tell me what you see.”
“The first three men died on Fridays each at a two week interval. When did Mary FitzPaulding die? Three days ago.”
“Also a Friday,” added Mr BonHomme, showing that he was awake.
“That means”, said Mr Hathaway, “that in less than two weeks someone else will die.”
“Finally, we agree on something.”

Chapter 5: Canterbury and its Cathedral

As they approached Canterbury, there were more and more people on the road, on foot, next to wagons and carts, and in carriages. Some people were leaving the city, having sold their goods. Others were travelling to the city after a day spent in hunting or some other activity. There were also pilgrims who came to the city for religious reasons. Canterbury had become a site for pilgrimages.
Even from a distance they could see Canterbury Cathedral rising up over the city walls, reaching towards heaven. Smoke rose from buildings as well. Canterbury had a population of around 10,000, which put it at about half the size of London. Amongst the population were Benedictine monks, some of whom moved freely throughout the city, dressed in their monastic robes.

Übung 34: Übersetzen Sie!

ÜBUNG 34 !

1. Die Hathaways und Mr BonHomme reisten mit der Kutsche.

2. Sie hofften, in Canterbury einige Informationen über Linus Groenig zu bekommen.

____

3. Mr Groenig war das erste Opfer des Mörders.

____

4. James de Bruyere und Linus Groenig wurden beide erstochen.

____

5. Canterbury war ungefähr halb so groß wie London.

____

Passing through the city walls, Mr Hathaway said, "You are about to experience Canterbury, BonHomme. Let's see what we find."

"I can hardly wait," BonHomme responded dryly.

The traffic in Canterbury was not nearly that of London. The streets were certainly not empty, however. The carriage driver guided the horse through the streets, past carts and wagons, to the inn where the Hathaways and Mr BonHomme were to spend at least one night. They were immediately shown to their rooms where they changed for dinner. After dinner they walked the streets of Canterbury briefly, but it was dark and they were tired so they returned to the inn. There they sat up in front of a fire until late.

Mrs Hathaway was the first to go to bed, because she wanted to get away from Mr BonHomme. "Mr BonHomme, indeed," she said to herself. "He may be a good man, I do not know, but he is not someone I enjoy being around."

Übung 35: Bilden Sie zu den folgenden Substantiven das passende Verb!

ÜBUNG 35 !

1. experience ______________________
2. guide ______________________
3. approach ______________________
4. death ______________________
5. speech ______________________
6. belief ______________________
7. company ______________________

The following morning after breakfast, the three went out onto the streets of Canterbury. As they walked into the city centre they came across markets where food and livestock were sold.
In the streets they heard people talking about God and prayers they were going to offer St Benedict or Mary or some other holy person. Canterbury Cathedral, with its tall spire, was a large building. What existed had taken a long time to complete, and it had been the site of at least one historical event.

Übung 36: Setzen Sie die Präpositionen in Klammern ein!
(in, on, by, from (2x), of, to, for)

ÜBUNG 36 !

"Here Thomas Beckett was murdered (1.) ________ knights hoping to please the king," Mr Hathaway said (2.) ________ Mr BonHomme. "That explains the pilgrims," the other added.

They entered the cathedral which contained many pilgrims but was not at all full. The ceiling was high and the walls appeared brown (3.) ______ many places. There were woodcarvings as well as painted scenes (4.) ______ the Bible. (5.) ______ the paintings (6.) ______ the wall, a favourite of Mr Hathaway was St. Paul and the Viper. Stained glass windows showed scenes (7.) ______ the Old and New Testaments for people who could not read and a series of windows told of miracles which had occurred near the grave of Thomas Beckett. Wooden benches were there (8.) ______ those who could afford them and open space for the rest.

The sounds of prayers, of people chanting and talking quietly, of people walking, filled the air. It was, in a word, noisy. They wandered around the church, observing the spectacle. Finally they came to an older man, dressed in black, who "seemed to belong to the place," as Mrs Hathaway later described it.
"We are here for some information," Mr Hathaway began.
The man examined them carefully before speaking. "What precisely do you want to know. If you want to know about the Order of St. Benedict, then I am the right person."
"We are looking for baptismal records."
"Let me get someone who can help you," said the man, and slowly disappeared among the pilgrims. A few minutes later he returned with a man not much younger. "He can help you," said the man and once again left them.
The newcomer introduced himself as Leonhard Smythe. "I manage records here at Canterbury Cathedral."

His voice is as dry as the papers he cares for, thought Mrs Hathaway, but she said nothing.

Übung 37: Vervollständigen Sie die Sätze mit den Wörtern in Klammern!
(prayer, chanting, spectacle, baptism, record, pilgrim)

1. An event which attracts public attention is a ________________.
2. A person who travels to a sacred place for religious reasons is a ________________.
3. A religious rite to become a member of the Christian Church is called a ________________.
4. Giving thanks to God or asking for His forgiveness is called a ________________.
5. A document giving an account of something that has happened is a ________________.
6. People singing psalms in a church are ________________.

"Good morning. I am Mr John Hathaway, this is Mr Harold BonHomme and this is my wife, Mrs Anna Hathaway. We are here from London because we are seeking information on two people."
"Why do you want this information? Are they relations of yours or have they committed some act against you?"
"No, indeed," Mr Hathaway answered. "Their fate was quite different. You see, they have both been murdered."

"Follow me," said Mr Smythe. He led them out of the cathedral proper and took them to the cathedral treasury where records were stored. Mrs Hathaway followed behind and remained in the background the whole time. She did not want to attract the man's attention. Perhaps she would not be allowed to stay with her husband and Mr BonHomme, she thought.

Übung 38: Setzen Sie die Verben in die richtige Zeitform!

"You are not a monk?" Mr BonHomme (1. ask) ________________.

"No. I am what is called an *oblate,* meaning I participate in much that takes place at the monastery but I am not a monk." They (2. enter) ________________ a large, dark room where the air (3. be) ________________ thick and old, and Mr Smythe continued, "We (4. keep) ________________ the records here. These books go back more than 500 years. So, who are we looking for and do you know approximately how long ago they (5. be) ________________ born?"

"The first person", said Mr Hathaway, "was Geoffrey de Kronung. He was perhaps as old as 25 but no older."

The man (6. pull) ________________ out a large, leather-bound book and paged back to 1290.

"Here's a Mary de Kronung. We can (7. come) ________________ back to this one if we cannot find Geoffrey de Kronung," he said and (8. run) ________________ his finger along the list of names that went down the right-hand side of the page. He (9. go) ________________ to 1289 and finally at 1288 he came across Geoffrey de Kronung. "Here we are," he said, a smile on his face. "2 June 1288 he was (10. baptize) ________________, which means he was born a few days earlier. You say he died this year? Then he was only 24 or about to turn 24. How sad."

"The parents are listed no doubt?" Mrs Hathaway said, trying to make her voice sound a bit masculine.
Mr Hathaway turned to look at her as did Mr Smythe.
"Yes, they are listed here. Martin and Susanne de Kronung."
"They do not list her name before she got married."
"Usually it is here, but in this case no name is listed."
"The other name", Mr Hathaway said, "is Linus Groenig. I am not sure how it is spelled."
"I remember seeing it a few minutes ago." His thumb went back up the list, to 1289 and then to 1290 – "Linus Groenig."
"Are his parents listed?"
"His mother is listed. A Miriam Groenig."
"Why is no father listed?"
"Well", Mr Smythe answered, "the father might have died before the child was born or the child might have been born of parents who were not married."
"Out of wedlock?" Mr BonHomme asked.
"Precisely. It is more common than you think, and I have seen many pregnant brides," Mr Smythe said matter-of-factly.
Mrs Hathaway turned bright red.

"Excuse me," Mr Smythe said. "I was not thinking."
"My wife is strong," Mr Hathaway said with a smile at his wife and then at Mr Smythe.

Übung 39: Übersetzen sie die folgenden Ausdrücke ins Englische!

1. unehelich geboren werden

____

2. in einem Verzeichnis gelistet sein

____

3. mit einem Mann verheiratet werden

____

4. knallrot werden

____

5. in einer Kirche getauft werden

____

"How can we find out the maiden name of Geoffrey de Kronung's mother?"
"We will have to look it up in the records of marriages," Mr Smythe answered.
"That is in a different book?" Mr Hathaway asked.
"It is. Fortunately, it is also here in this archive."
He put the record of baptisms back in its place on the shelf and went off to get the book in which marriages were recorded. This book was just as big and heavy as the first one. It did not take long for Mr

Smythe to find the date of the wedding for Martin and Susanne de Kronung, moving backwards from the date of the baptism of Geoffrey de Kronung.

"It's not listed here," Mr Smythe said.

"What do you mean?" Mr Hathaway asked.

"Her maiden name, her name before she got married, it isn't listed here. That is quite strange. It has to be here, really. How could it be that it was not recorded?" Mr Smythe appeared to be truly amazed.

Übung 40: Beantworten Sie die Fragen zum Text!

1. Who is Leonard Smythe?

____

2. Why are the Hathaways and Mr BonHomme at Canterbury Cathedral?

____

3. What may be a reason why Linus Groenig's father isn't listed in the church records?

____

4. Why does Mrs Hathaway turn bright red?

____

5. Why isn't Leonard Smythe able to find the maiden name of Geoffrey de Kronung's mother?

____

"She paid to keep it out," Mr BonHomme suggested. "Either Susanne de Kronung or her husband."
Mr Smythe turned to Mr BonHomme and gave him a look of strong disapproval. "That would go against the church's own rules," he declared. "It's impossible that the church would commit such an act."
"Then how do you explain it?" Mr BonHomme asked.
"I can't."
"Well –" Mr BonHomme began but was interrupted.
"It is not important how it happened," Mrs Hathaway said. "What is important is how do we get this information? What other way is there to get such information?"
"I can only think that there must be someone in Canterbury polite society who would know their whereabouts," Mr Smythe said.
"Would you be willing to put us in touch with someone who would help us get access to this person?" Mrs Hathaway asked.

ÜBUNG 41 !

Übung 41: Lesen Sie weiter und unterstreichen Sie alle Adjektive im folgenden Textabschnitt!

"I am not so well-connected", Mr Smythe admitted, "but I know someone who could probably introduce you to the proper person or could at least provide you access to Canterbury society."
"Who?" Mr Hathaway asked.
In answer, Mr Smythe walked out of the room and returned ten minutes later with a Benedictine monk of about 40 or 45, who wore dark brown robes, had a beard cut short and eyes that seemed as if they could see through words to the truth. Brother Ephraim was quite well-known in Canterbury high society. Educated and comfortable discussing subjects sometimes considered controversial,

Brother Ephraim was frequently invited to dinner with one or another of the more important families in Canterbury.

"What can I do for you?" Brother Ephraim asked, once the introductions were completed.
Mr Hathaway immediately explained to Brother Ephraim the circumstances of their journey to Canterbury. "There have been several murders, by the same person we think, and we want to see if they are in some way connected."
"A constable has sent you here, then?" Brother Ephraim asked.
"No. A person I counted amongst my friends has become a victim of the murderer."
"You want revenge?"
"No. Four people have now been murdered, and I want it to stop."
"And how do you plan on stopping it?"
"We think, Brother Ephraim", said Mrs Hathaway, "that there is some connection between the people he has murdered, a connection that we simply cannot see just yet."
"Why do you think there is a connection?"
"Four people have been murdered, two with a sword, one strangled and a fourth with poison. Each body has been found with the little finger missing."

Übung 42: Formulieren Sie die Sätze im Passiv!

ÜBUNG 42 !

1. The constable didn't send them to Canterbury.

____

2. The murderer killed four people.

____

3. They completed the introductions.

4. Smythe introduced them to Brother Ephraim.

5. Mrs Hathaway explained the circumstances to Brother Ephraim.

Brother Ephraim made the sign of the cross but said nothing.
"Two of the victims, a Geoffrey de Kronung and Linus Groenig, come from Canterbury. There is little information on them, however. We were hoping to get background information on the families of the two. Unfortunately, we know nothing about the families of Martin de Kronung or his wife Susanne. Only a mother is listed for Linus Groenig's baptism."
"I can put you in contact with someone who may know about de Kronung, if anyone will. I do not know about Linus Groenig." He stopped for a moment, stared out the window and then added, "Meet me here after we have prayed None. I will see if I can arrange something in the meantime." After a moment, he added, "I cannot guarantee anything. I know one woman who might be willing to speak to you, but I promise nothing. She is discrete and I will explain why you want the information you need, but I do not know whether she will be…informative."
They agreed to meet later and so Mr and Mrs Hathaway and Mr BonHomme left, after thanking Mr Smythe and Brother Ephraim. As the day was warm, they walked the streets of Canterbury and then went to an inn for lunch. Afterwards they returned to their rooms and rested and then changed their clothing before returning to Canterbury Cathedral.

Chapter 6: In Canterbury Society

They left their rooms around the middle of the afternoon and walked slowly. They were dressed for the evening, in case they should not be able to return to their rooms before dinner. The day had not darkened at all, as was frequently the case at Canterbury. It is not far from the ocean, so the weather can change quickly and dramatically. Citizens and visitors must be prepared for all kinds of weather. Mr and Mrs Hathaway were not prepared for such unusually nice weather. Mr Hathaway was enjoying the weather, while his wife was quiet and deep in thought. Mr BonHomme, too, kept to himself.

"What do you think of Canterbury, BonHomme?"

"It is not too bad," Mr BonHomme admitted.

The two men discussed the general merits of Canterbury, while Mrs Hathaway followed.

Übung 43: Simple Present oder Present Progressive (Verlaufsform)? Setzen Sie die passende Form ein!

1. The weather in Canterbury usually (change) ______________ quickly.
2. Mr Hathaway (walk) ______________ slowly now.
3. What are they doing? They (thank) ______________ Brother Ephraim for his help.
4. Mrs Hathaway (love) ______________ her husband deeply.

5. Mr Hathaway always thinks his wife (look) ______________ beautiful.

6. At the moment, she (observe) ______________ Mr BonHomme.

A man about the same age as Hathaway, but obviously of the poorer classes, jumped out at them. "So what are you doing here?"
Mr Hathaway stopped quickly and looked the man in the face. His hair was curly and wild and his face was dirty. "Are you looking for Jesus or his Mother? Well, you won't find them here – ha, ha, ha."
His clothes were dirty and dirty skin was visible through the holes.
Mr Hathaway attempted to go around him but the man stopped him.
"Are you seeking truths?"
"I am seeking to go around you, if you want to know," Mr Hathaway said.
"You can only go through me," he responded.
Mr BonHomme walked quickly over to the man and pushed him so forcefully that he should have fallen to the ground. He managed, however, to stay on his feet. All three men suddenly had weapons out, long knives called 'daggers'.
"Stand back, BonHomme," said Mr Hathaway.
"Good man, good man," said the stranger and began to circle around Mr Hathaway.

ÜBUNG 44 !

Übung 44: Adverb oder Adjektiv? Setzen Sie die Adjektive in Klammern in die richtige Form!

Mrs Hathaway was now out of her dream-state and rather (1. fearful) ______________ watching her husband, holding on to Mr

BonHomme's arm. A (2. small) ______________ crowd had gathered to watch. The stranger jumped at Mr Hathaway several times. He was attempting to (3. serious) ________________ hurt him and not playing at all. He tried once again and, with his fist, Mr Hathaway knocked the dagger out of his hand. The stranger did not back away, however. He suddenly tried to jump on Mr Hathaway. He grabbed hold of both of Mr Hathaway's hands and pushed him backwards. Mr Hathaway fell backwards and then turned to the side, pushing the stranger past him. Even more (4. forceful) _______________ than Mr BonHomme he pushed the stranger away and then kicked him. This time, the stranger fell to the ground and rolled onto his back like a turtle.

"Get out of here," Mr Hathaway yelled. "Get up and get out of here."

Some in the crowd were (5. unhappy) _______________ with the result, shouting "You should have killed him!" and "What do you have against a (6. good) _______________ fight?" and more.

"Dagger, BonHomme," Mr Hathaway said, and Mr BonHomme retrieved the stranger's dagger while Mr Hathaway watched the man limp away. "That, my dear, was a madman," Mr Hathaway said to his wife. "I should have preferred to fight him with a sword, but then I might have been forced to kill him."

"You handled yourself well," said Mrs Hathaway.

"I must practice a bit with a sword. I have a duel to fight with Constable Warwicke at some time in the future."

"Why?" asked Mrs Hathaway, unhappily.

"We have a difference of opinion."

"I would be quite willing to be your second at the duel", Mr Bon-Homme said, "and we could practice with swords, too. I am not a great swordsman, but I believe I can help you practice."

They made their way to Canterbury Cathedral where Brother Ephraim was waiting.

"Has something happened?" Brother Ephraim asked.

"No – yes. We met a local person, I assume, who is a madman."

"I hope he was not too much trouble."

"No, he just showed me that I have to be better prepared."

"I am going to take you to a Mrs Mary Marklan," he said. "She should be able to help you or will know someone who can."

! ÜBUNG 45

*Übung 45: **Who** oder **which**?*
Markieren Sie mit richtig ✔ oder falsch –!

1. Mr Hathaway fought with somebody which was a madman. ☐
2. Mrs Hathaway loved her husband who respected her. ☐
3. It was Brother Ephraim who gave them the information. ☐
4. They wanted to find the person which murdered Groenig. ☐
5. They didn't like the Canterbury society who was very different from the London society. ☐
6. Many ideas which look good at first just don't work in practice. ☐

They came to an attractive building, with a stone roof, and Brother Ephraim knocked. They were allowed in and taken to a room where they were left alone for a moment. Soon a woman of about 55 entered the room. She was white-haired and yet her face did not look so old. After the greetings and introductions, they sat down and drank a glass of sweet wine.

“Brother Ephraim tells me you are here on unpleasant business,” she began.

“Unpleasant but necessary business,” Mr Hathaway said. “There have been several murders in London –”

“Really an unpleasant city,” she interrupted.

“There are parts that are not pleasant”, Mr Hathaway agreed, “but it has its advantages.”

“I do not know what they are,” she returned.

“We are here, Mrs Marklan”, said Mrs Hathaway, “because a friend of ours was murdered. We are hoping you might have some information about a Geoffrey de Kronung or a family named de Kronung.”

Übung 46: Bilden Sie aus den folgenden bejahten Aussagesätzen verneinte Aussagesätze!

1. The building had a straw roof.

____

2. He thought that London was a boring city.

____

3. Somebody was able to help them.

____

4. Mr BonHomme wanted to be Mr Hathaway’s second at the duel.

____

5. He was murdered by a madman.

---

6. She knew somebody with the name 'de Kronung'.

Mrs Marklan turned to look at Mrs Hathaway and examined her quite closely. She seemed to be trying to decide if she should respond to what the younger woman had said. Finally she spoke, "Yes, I know of the de Kronungs, but Geoffrey's parents, Martin and Susanne are both dead now. An illness, that we were afraid was a plague, killed them. It took them very quickly only a few years ago."
"Geoffrey is now dead as well."
"Yes, he was ambitious and went to London to make his fortune."
"Do you know anything about their family?"
"De Kronung is a family of long-standing here in Canterbury. They are a noble family; however, they have some connections with the merchant class."
"That is unusual."
"They were unusual people. By the way, Geoffrey had two brothers, Martin and Arthur, and a sister Mary. They are still here."

ÜBUNG 47 !

Übung 47: Lesen Sie weiter und unterstreichen Sie die richtige Variante!

"Do you know (1.) something/anything about the background of Susanne de Kronung?"
"Yes. She was a Childe, daughter (2.) of/from Harold Childe. She did not want anything to do with her family and when the rest of

them left (3.) to/for London she stayed behind in Canterbury. As a daughter she had nothing to inherit and the dowry, the money her father gave her husband at her wedding, was quite small. She was a lively girl and a strong-willed young woman. She remained that way all her life. About thirty years (4.) before/ago something happened that split the entire Childe family. I do not know what it (5.) was/has been, but (6.) anything/something happened."

"You have no idea what happened or you are not willing to tell us?"

"I have no idea," she answered.

"What about Linus Groenig?" Mr Hathaway asked. "Have you (7.) ever/never heard of him? You see, in the baptism records only his mother is listed."

"That happens sometimes," Mrs Marklan said with a look that was almost cold.

"I think", said Brother Ephraim, speaking for the first time in a while, "Mr Smythe explained that."

"He explained nothing," Mr Hathaway said, looking surprised. "At least nothing specific to Linus Groenig."

"Do you know anything about him?" Mrs Hathaway asked.

Mrs Marklan thought for a moment. "No, that name does not seem familiar. If you would like to stay to dinner", she continued, "I have some guests who may know something about the people you are interested in."

"That's very kind of you, Mrs Marklan," said Mrs Hathaway, happy that she had planned ahead and was appropriately dressed for dinner.

"We would be very grateful," said Mr Hathaway.

Brother Ephraim left soon after and returned to the monastery.

ÜBUNG 48 !

Übung 48: Setzen Sie die Wörter in die richtige Reihenfolge und bilden Sie sinnvolle Fragesätze!

1. know do anything Kronungs about you the de

___

2. family the does have the class with merchant connections

___

3. Kronung did the background of say Susanne about de she anything

___

4. for you like to dinner would stay

___

5. to brought Canterbury you what

___

6. murdered why want do to find out him who you

___

Several hours later, after an enjoyable dinner, when everyone was sitting around in candlelight, Mrs Marklan brought up the topic of great interest to the Hathaways.

"My dear Mrs Otsworth, these pleasant young people have come from London about something that I did not wish to discuss over dinner. There have been several murders in London, and they are trying to stop them."

Mrs Otsworth was over 60, fat, and she had a big pile of hair on her head. She turned on the Londoners a look that contained a mixture of interest and disgust. Her large eyes grew even larger and she stared at the Hathaways, making them uncomfortable.

"If the murders are in London", she began, speaking quite slowly, "why did you come to Canterbury?"

"Because", Mr Hathaway answered, "two of the victims came from Canterbury."

"Did they indeed?" she asked.

Mr Hathaway nodded in answer.

"How unfortunate," she added.

"One was named Geoffrey de Kronung," Mr Hathaway added.

"Oh," Mrs Otsworth cried out suddenly, waking her even older husband. "I heard that he had been murdered. And you want to find out who murdered him? We knew his mother, though not very well. She tended to keep out of society. I hope you find his murderer."

Übung 49: Welche Wörter haben eine ähnliche Bedeutung?

1. respond	☐ aversion
2. ambitious	☐ answer
3. fortune	☐ suitable
4. merchant	☐ wealth
5. remain	☐ determined
6. appropriate	☐ stack
7. pile	☐ salesman
8. disgust	☐ stay

"Do you know why she didn't mix in society?" Mr Hathaway asked.

"She must have had her reasons."

"No doubt. Do you know what they were?" Mrs Hathaway asked, speaking for the first time since dinner.

Mrs Otsworth turned to Mrs Hathaway and studied her a moment, silently. “There were rumours of a scandal and it must have been this scandal that divided the Childe household. You see, about half the family wanted nothing more to do with their father, Harold Childe. Susanne, Philip and Clotilde Childe cut themselves off from their father. Young Harold and Claude sided with their father. Another son, Bruce, did as well, but he died soon after.”
“Do you know what sort of scandal it was?” Mr Hathaway asked, when she had stopped speaking.
“No. We were in London when it happened and details were never known.”
“That must have been difficult to keep secret,” Mr BonHomme said.
“It must have been,” agreed Mrs Otsworth, smiling.
“Have you ever heard of a Linus Groenig?” Mr Hathaway asked, when it was clear Mrs Otsworth was not going to reveal anything else about the Childe scandal.

ÜBUNG 50 !

Übung 50: Wie heißt das Simple Past und das Past Participle der folgenden Verben?

1. hear ______ ______
2. be ______ ______
3. cut ______ ______
4. see ______ ______
5. fight ______ ______
6. keep ______ ______

7. grow ______________ ______________

8. speak ______________ ______________

"He worked in the de Kronung household as a young lad, I think, but I am not sure about that. You would have to speak with old Maria, the former family servant –"
"Yes, old Maria –" said Mrs Marklan.
"She must be very old, indeed, if she is not dead. But she could tell you something about the Childe family, too, I am certain."
"Can you help us locate her?" asked Mr Hathaway.
"I am sure one of my servants knows her whereabouts. Come to my house tomorrow morning and I'll give you what information I can."

Übung 51: Ersetzen Sie den Satzteil in Klammern durch eine Infinitivkonstruktion!

ÜBUNG 51 !

1. London is the place (where you should live) *to live*.

2. Mr Hathaway was not the type (who would give up)

______________.

3. Was Mr Smythe a man (who could be trusted) ______________?

4. They were looking for a place (where they could stay)

______________.

5. She wanted someone (for whom she could care) ______________.

6. Mr BonHomme was the only one (who disliked Canterbury)

______________.

Chapter 7: Visiting the Old Servant

The following morning, Mr and Mrs Hathaway took their carriage to Mrs Otsworth's house. Mr BonHomme decided that he wanted to walk around Canterbury on his own. It was a good thing, too, because the tension between Mrs Hathaway and Mr BonHomme had been growing since the beginning of the journey.

"You look ravishing, *Mrs* Hathaway," Mr Hathaway said to his wife as they stepped out of the inn.

"Why, thank you, *Mr* Hathaway" she answered, turning red. "I feel relaxed for the first time since we left London."

"And the weather is so lovely again today. It almost seems as if it is a spring or summer day."

! ÜBUNG 52

Übung 52: Lesen Sie weiter und unterstreichen Sie das richtige Wort!

"If only we had the day to (1.) ourselves/themselves. We could go for a ride or a walk (2.) on/in the countryside to really enjoy the (3.) weather/whether. This might be the last nice day for months."

She stopped speaking for a moment and (4.) then/than asked, "Do you think old Maria will speak to us?"

"If she speaks to anyone, she will speak to you. You will (5.) have to/must go in first and do most of the talking."

"Perhaps. But sometimes these older women like younger men. It (6.) might/can be your charm that gets us access to the information we need."

"We will just have to wait and see and take things (7.) as/like they come."

At Mrs Otsworth's house they and their driver were given directions to old Maria's house, Maria Brown. They were warned that her daughter was a bit protective. If they said that Jennie Buckley sent them, however, they would probably have no problem getting past her and to her mother.
"Who is Jennie Buckley?" Mrs Hathaway asked.
"She is my family servant. Naturally, we have more than one, but she has been here the longest and she runs everything."
They thanked Mrs Otsworth for her help and were then on their way. "We do not want to inconvenience you any further," Mr Hathaway said, firmly turning down an invitation to lunch.
"Well, you need not lunch here", Mrs Otsworth said, somewhat displeased, "if it does not meet your standards."
"We would love to lunch with you", Mrs Hathaway said, "but it is a question of time. We have much to do before we return to London tomorrow. Time is very important at the moment."

*Übung 53: Setzen Sie jeweils **must/mustn't** oder **have to/don't have to** in die Lücke ein!*

1. You ________________ lunch here, if you don't want to.
2. You ________________ mess with a madman!
3. They ________________ go to Canterbury to get more information.
4. A family servant ________________ be loyal.
5. I like helping you. You ________________ thank me.

The driver followed the directions as best he could, but they still managed to get lost a couple of times. Finally, getting directions from

someone on foot, they found old Maria's house. It was a three-storey house in a row of other such houses and the street was littered with all types of waste. Mrs Hathaway held up a perfumed handkerchief to her nose when the smell became too much for her. After knocking several times and getting no response, Mr Hathaway knocked harder and the door opened. No one was there, so he led Mrs Hathaway in.
"Hello, Mrs Brown," he called out once and then a second time.
After a moment, there was a noise on the second floor. "Who's yelling and making all that noise?" a woman's voice called out. "My baby's trying to sleep."
"We are looking for Maria Brown," said Mr Hathaway.
"Well, go on up, then. She lives at the top. She won't be coming down to meet you. She can't. She can't take the steps anymore."
Mr and Mrs Hathaway took the advice and went up the stairs to the very top. Once there they saw an angry-looking woman staring at them.

ÜBUNG 54 !

Übung 54: Simple Past oder Verlaufsform? Setzen Sie die Verben in Klammern in die richtige Form!

1. After (knock) ________________ at the door, they (get) ________________ a response from inside.
2. Though (follow) ________________ the directions from the Hathaways, the driver (get lost) ________________ a couple times.
3. She (hate) ________________ him for (be) ________________ so boring.
4. They (go) ________________ to Mary Brown's house without (hesitate) ________________.

5. After (climb) ________________ the stairs, they (see) ________________ an angry looking woman.

"And what do you want with my mother?"
"Jennie Buckley sent us," Mr Hathaway began.
"Did she? Well, what do you want with my mother? She's not so healthy anymore, so she won't be working for you."
Mrs Hathaway pushed in front of her husband. She had put her handkerchief away. "We are here because we would like to ask her a few questions about the de Kronungs."
"They died seven years ago and thank God she didn't die with them," the woman answered. "She's not in the best of health and doesn't need to be answering a lot of questions."
"Let them in," an old and yet fairly strong voice called out.
The woman stepped out of their way and motioned for them to walk in. "It's not what you're used to," she said.
"You do not know what we are used to," Mrs Hathaway said gently, entering first.

Übung 55: Übersetzen Sie und enträtseln Sie das Lösungswort!

ÜBUNG 55 !

1. gesund ☐ _ _ _ _ _ _
2. Abfall _ ☐ _ _ _
3. Einladung _ ☐ _ _ _ _ _ _ _ _
4. Ratschlag _ ☐ _ _ _ _
5. Spaziergang _ _ _ ☐
6. sanft _ ☐ _ _ _ _

7. Hausangestellter _ _ ☐ _ _ _ _

8. Unbequemlichkeit _ _ ☐ _ _ _ _ _ _ _ _ _ _

9. Charme _ ☐ _ _ _

10. Anweisungen _ ☐ _ _ _ _ _ _ _ _ _

11. schreien _ ☐ _ _

12. Parfum _ _ _ ☐ _ _ _

Lösung: _ _ _ _ _ _ _ _ _ _ _ _ _

Despite the brightness of the day, there was not much light in the room. No candles were burning, however, and no fire was lit. The room was small and Maria Brown was sitting in a bed which was on the floor. She looked alert and watched them as they entered the small room.

"I don't know you," she said.

"No, you do not," Mrs Hathaway agreed.

"My daughter is always trying to send my visitors away."

"You haven't had a visitor in years, Mother."

"So you shouldn't be sending these away," she said, without anger.

"So, what can I do for you?" she asked.

"We are here to ask you some questions about the de Kronungs."

"I worked there for years."

"Were they nice people?"

"Nice enough," Maria Brown answered. "Better than most, I reckon. They almost always treated me with respect."

"Could you tell me about Mrs de Kronung, about her family?" Mrs Hathaway asked.

"The de Kronungs were her family."

"But she was born a Childe."

"When I knew her she was not a Childe anymore."

Übung 56: Welcher Fragesatz ist richtig formuliert? Kreuzen Sie an!

1. Woran starb sie?
   a) ☐ Why did she die?
   b) ☐ Of what did she die?
   c) ☐ What did she die of?

2. Für wen arbeitete Mr de Kronung?
   a) ☐ What did Mr de Kronung work for?
   b) ☐ For who did Mr de Kronung work?
   c) ☐ Who did Mr de Kronung work for?

3. Kennen Sie Linus Groenig?
   a) ☐ Know you Linus Groenig?
   b) ☐ Do you know Linus Groenig?
   c) ☐ Who knows Linus Groenig?

4. Zu wem gingen Sie letzte Nacht?
   a) ☐ To who did you go last night?
   b) ☐ Who did you go to last night?
   c) ☐ Whom did you go to last night?

"Why was that?"
"She was married."
"Now Mrs Brown", Mrs Hathaway said, as if hurt by this response, "you know that is not what I meant."
"I can't tell you any more."
"You cannot or will not?" Mr Hathaway asked.
"What's the difference, young man?"
"They died seven years ago, your daughter said," Mrs Hathaway continued. "Do you know what they died of?"

"The physician thought it might have been plague at first, but if it was they were the only ones who died of it."

ÜBUNG 57

Übung 57: Setzen Sie die Verben in Klammern in die richtige Zeitform!

Mrs Brown's daughter (1. come) ______________ out with four small tin cups and (2. pour) ______________ a sweet wine into them and handed them around. She (3. appear) ______________ much more pleasant suddenly. The day was still nice and yet seemed to be darkening in the room. Small windows looked out onto the street.

"Are you sure they (4. die) ______________ of an illness?"

"What else could it've been?" the old woman asked.

"Do you (5. remember) ______________ Geoffrey de Kronung?" Mr Hathaway asked.

"Yes, of course."

Mrs Hathaway (6. put) ______________ her hand on Mr Hathaway's arm and he stopped speaking.

"Do you (7. know) ______________ Linus Groenig?" she asked.

"Do I know him? He was a cheeky lad. He was always acting as if he were better than he was."

"Did he (8. work) ______________ for the de Kronungs."

"He did and he didn't. He wasn't an employee but he wasn't the same as Geoffrey. He had a small room at the top of the house. I heard that after the deaths of the de Kronungs he went to London with Geoffrey. He was supposed to work with Geoffrey, but it didn't turn out well and he started working for someone else. He transported goods between Canterbury and London."

"So they were not friends or brothers?"

"They were certainly not brothers, and they only tolerated each other. I thought some day that they might end up as brothers, because brothers always fight. But as I said, the last I heard he was working for someone in London. Besides, Geoffrey had an older brother, Martin, and a younger brother Arthur. What did he need another brother for?"

Übung 58: Sind die folgenden Aussagen richtig? Markieren Sie mit richtig ✓ oder falsch – !

ÜBUNG 58 !

1. Jennie Buckley was Mrs Otsworth's servant. ☐
2. Geoffrey de Kronung and his family died seven years ago. ☐
3. Mary Brown was a servant for the de Kronungs. ☐
4. Mrs de Kronung was born Groenig. ☐
5. Mrs Brown didn't know for sure what the de Kronung family died of. ☐
6. Linus Groenig lived with the de Kronungs. ☐
7. Linus Groenig and Geoffrey de Kronung went to London together. ☐

"Do you know anything about Linus Groenig's father?"

"I was told that his name was Phip. I don't know any more – no one knew any more. The one time I heard Linus's mother mention Phip, Mrs de Kronung asked her not to speak of him. In any case, his mother quite loved this Phip. She said that Linus had some of his father's nobility, but I never saw it. He was a good boy, mind you – good but cheeky, which is why he didn't get on with Geoffrey."

"Did Linus Groenig's mother work in the de Kronung house?"

"Absolutely not," old Mary said, getting upset. "She was no good for work. She was just a pretty whore, no more. She was like Linus, always acting as if she were better than the rest of us."

"Where is she now?" Mr Hathaway asked.

"In a pauper's graveyard where she belongs." Mary Brown looked up at them. "Why are you asking so many questions about these boys?"

ÜBUNG 59

Übung 59: Ergänzen Sie die Sätze mit den Wörtern in Klammern!
(cheeky, protective, plague, employee, pauper)

1. A deadly disease spreading rapidly over a wide area is called a __________________.
2. A person working in return for payment is an __________________.
3. A __________________ person is lacking the proper respect.
4. A poor person can be called a __________________.
5. A __________________ person keeps another person safe.

Mrs Brown's daughter coughed and gave the signal not to answer when Mr and Mrs Hathaway looked up at her.

"Mrs Brown", Mrs Hathaway began, looking up at the daughter helplessly, "they are dead. We are trying to find out who killed them and why."

Mrs Brown let out a cry of shock and began crying.

"Now why'd you have to go and tell her that?" her daughter asked. "I've kept it from her now more than three months. She was happier not knowing it."
"It is the truth," Mrs Hathaway answered. "Two other people have also died by the same killer. We are trying to stop someone from killing more people and that is why we are here asking questions. There is some reason behind the choice of victims, and we are trying to work out what it is."
"Well, she won't be able to talk to you anymore today," the daughter said.

Übung 60: Setzen Sie die fehlenden Personal- und Possessivpronomen ein!

! ÜBUNG 60

Mrs Hathaway leaned over the old woman and comforted (1.) __________ for a moment. When (2.) __________ stood up, she and Mr Hathaway left.
"Goodbye, Mrs Brown," they said. Just outside (3.) __________ also said goodbye to her daughter and Mr Hathaway gave (4.) __________ some money.
"Thank you", he said to her, "and I am heartily sorry to have caused (5.) __________ such trouble."
"(6.) __________ can't accept that," she said.
"For your trouble," (7.) __________ answered with a friendly smile, closing the hand that held the coins.

They walked down the stairs and outside found (8.) __________ carriage surrounded by a gang of boys and girls.

"Get away," their driver was shouting. "Go back to the dirt (9.) __________ came from."

"In God's name, what is going on here?" asked Mr Hathaway, and the children suddenly moved away to let the Hathaways through.
"I'll run you down with the horses if any of you get in the way," the driver threatened, as the children looked on.
"That is not necessary," Mr Hathaway said. "They will not be getting in the way or under the wheels."

Chapter 8: Martin de Kronung's Warning

Following Mr Hathaway's orders, the driver drove the carriage to Mrs Marklan's house. There they briefly sat with her and drank something warm, made of a mixture of herbs and spices, before getting directions to Martin de Kronung's house.
"Though he was named after his father, he is not at all like his father – or his mother, for that matter," Mrs Marklan warned but would not explain any further.
"What does he think of the Childes," Mrs Hathaway asked.
"He is not close to them either, I believe," she answered.
"Do you know why?"
"He may not have sought them out, or they may have rejected him – after all, he has the blood of his mother in his veins and she rejected the Childes."
"Do you think he will speak with us?"
"I do not see why not. He may not answer your questions, though."

Übung 61: Simple Past oder Past Perfect? Setzen Sie das Verb in Klammern in die passende Zeitform!

1. They (just leave) ______________________ Mrs Otsworth when the carriage got lost.
2. An hour later, they (talk) ______________________ to Mrs Brown and her daughter.
3. They found the Browns' house after someone on foot (give) ______________________ them the directions.
4. The night before they visited Mrs. Brown, they (stay) ______________________ at an inn.
5. They (visit) ______________________ Mrs Marklan after they left Mary Brown.

Martin de Kronung's house was not far from Mrs Marklan's. It was a big house with something grand and noble about it. The Hathaways were immediately welcomed in but were made to wait more than ten minutes before Mr de Kronung came to them. He was younger than the Hathaways, no older than 27, but dressed elegantly, with brightly-coloured clothes. He studied the Hathaways a moment, as if judging their standing in society. His examination did not persuade him to behave in a more friendly fashion towards them.
After the introductions, Mr de Kronung ordered the servant to bring food and drink. While waiting, he came straight to the point. "So, what can I do for you?"
"We have come about your brother's murder," Mr Hathaway responded.

"That was months ago."
"Just over three months ago, and more have died since."

ÜBUNG 62 !

*Übung 62: Setzen Sie **for** oder **since** in die Lücken ein!*

1. Many people have died ________ the death of Geoffrey de Kronung.
2. The Hathaways have been in Canterbury ________ two days.
3. They have been up ________ the sun rose.
4. They haven't eaten anything ________ they had breakfast.
5. The driver has been waiting in his carriage ________ an hour.

"Really." The man did not look sad but only emotionless.
"Do you have any idea why anyone would want to murder your brother?"
"No, I do not," he answered. There was silence for a moment, as the Hathaways waited for something more. "I always told him", Mr de Kronung continued, "that he should not have lowered himself to work as a merchant and you see what has become of his decision."
"You think he was murdered because he went into business?"
"Why not?"
"It is quite clear that there was some other motivation", Mr Hathaway said, "because he was not robbed. He had a tidy sum of money on him when he was found."
"Well, that shows you what kind of a murderer you are looking for."
"I do not understand." Confused, Mr Hathaway looked from Mr de Kronung to his wife.

Übung 63: Unterstreichen Sie die englische Übersetzung der folgenden Wörter!
(1. gründlich, 2. Stille, 3. unangenehm, 4. Weile, 5. merkte, 6. Subjekt, 7. Zorn, 8. Trauer)

"He is either not thorough or he is rich," Mr de Kronung finally added.
"Or", said Mrs Hathaway, breaking her silence, "his motives have nothing to do with money."
Mr de Kronung looked at her and gave her an unpleasant smile. "Agreed."
"What can you tell us about Linus Groenig?"
"That little monkey that my parents allowed to grow up in our house? If he had not been murdered, I might have killed him myself. He worked with my brother for a while, until my brother, stupid as he was, finally realized that it was impossible to work with such a being. Even Geoffrey finally left Linus on his own."
"You do not seem to care very much that your brother is dead," Mrs Hathaway said, anger in her voice.
"I have done my mourning."

"You are no longer dressed for mourning," she said, referring to the bright colours of his clothing in place of the more traditional black of mourning. It was expected that mourning would go on for more than a few months, possibly up to a year.
"He rejected everything that I stand for," Mr de Kronung responded, raising his voice. "Do you understand that? I am a member of the aristocracy, and he went to London to become a simple merchant."
"He went to London to become more than a simple merchant," Mr Hathaway corrected. "His business was quite successful and was becoming even more so. He would have become quite wealthy, if his business had gone on as it was."

ÜBUNG 64 !

Übung 64: Setzen Sie die Wörter in die richtige Reihenfolge und bilden Sie sinnvolle Sätze!

1. Mr of Linus anger while de Kronung couldn't Groenig hide his speaking

____

2. brother de Kronung Mr thought his was murdered he into because went business

____

3. Groenig Linus ran a business successful London in

____

4. de Kronung Martin seem didn't be to grief-stricken very

____

5. Groenig if hadn't been he might murdered killed have him himself

____

"Business," Mr de Kronung spoke the word as if it were a vulgarity. "Business – do you hear yourself, Hathaway? My grandfather was a cousin of the king. My great-great grandfather was a brother of a king. Business is not for people like us. If we do anything, we *rule.*"
"Kings have many cousins, Mr de Kronung," Mr Hathaway said.
An ugly look came across Mr de Kronung's face for a moment. "Are you a cousin of the king?" he asked quietly.
"No, I am not," Mr Hathaway admitted without showing any sign of weakness.

"Then", Mr de Kronung's voice was quite controlled, "not everyone can claim to be a cousin. Do you have a sword?"
"I am not unarmed," Mr Hathaway answered, staring directly at Mr de Kronung. There was silence a moment.
"What did you come here for?" Mr de Kronung asked at last. "Did you only come here to insult me?"
"I did not come here to insult you –"

Übung 65: Lesen Sie weiter und unterstreichen Sie die richtige Variante!

"And (1.) yet/already you have succeeded."
"We came to ask (2.) if/whether you might know why someone would want to kill your brother."
"I (3.) had/have already answered that question. I said that I did not."
"Could you tell us (4.) from/about your brother, Arthur?"
"He is (5.) younger/more young and therefore a bit (6.) recklesser/ more reckless than I am."
There was a pause as the Hathaways (7.) thought/had thought about Mr de Kronung's words.
"There is a rumour that something (8.) has happened/happened in the Childe family thirty years ago," Mr Hathaway said.

"Rumours are like the smells you cannot help but notice in the street: they come from filth."
"You are a descendant of the Childe family. You must know something about your family history."
"My mother wanted nothing to do with the Childe family. She was free-spirited and broke many of the conventions of her time. When I tried to renew contact with them, they had no interest in the son of

Susanne Childe de Kronung." There was a certain bitterness in his voice that he could not hide.

"Do you know what it was that happened so many years ago?"

"I do not know, but if I did I would not tell you." The two men stared at each other. "I am sure you can find some old lady here in Canterbury who would be happy to tell you every single detail if only to avoid being bored for ten or twenty minutes."

! ÜBUNG 66

Übung 66: Haben die Wörter eine ähnliche Bedeutung? Markieren Sie mit richtig ✓ oder falsch – !

1. unarmed/unharmed ☐
2. claim/demand ☐
3. arms/weapons ☐
4. insult/offend ☐
5. rumour/noise ☐
6. filth/dirt ☐
7. descendant/ancestor ☐
8. convention/monastery ☐

"So far none of them has spoken to us."

"Perhaps someone paid them for their silence?" Mrs Hathaway added.

"I do not know. You see, I never met my grandfather, so I know nothing about him nor anything that happened thirty years ago. It would change nothing for me, if I did."

"There is nothing further to be gained here, my dear," Mr Hathaway said, standing up.

"I could not agree more," she answered, joining him.

Mr de Kronung stood up as well.

"Thank you for your time," Mr Hathaway said.
"Mr Hathaway", Mr de Kronung said, and his voice became even uglier than before, "if we ever meet again and you speak to me as you have today, be prepared to pay with your life."
"Mr de Kronung, on the field of bravery many noblemen have fallen. I am skilled in the use of language and in the use of swords. I have said nothing that I would not be quite happy to defend with my life. I do not wish to fight you with swords but I am not afraid of it."
"My mother said my brother was a de Kronung and that I was a Childe. And we Childes are brutal and heartless. We do not win or lose; we *take* – and we take what we want."

Übung 67: Lesen Sie weiter und unterstreichen Sie die fünf inhaltlich nicht dazugehörenden Sätze!

The door closed behind them and they got in their carriage and were gone. Then they fell asleep.
"What an arrogant man," Mrs Hathaway said. "I have met many proud and arrogant people, but I have never anyone quite so arrogant as he is. I think he is a true nobleman."
"It is because he is fighting for his reputation that he is so arrogant, my dear."
"He is very respectable. And he did not even seem to care that his brother was dead."
"They must have hated each other. Martin de Kronung does not see that as cities get larger, business will become more important. He likes being a merchant. Geoffrey de Kronung probably thought that he saw the future."
"I might almost think that brother had killed brother", said Mrs Hathaway, "if it were not for Mary FitzPaulding and James de

Bruyere. They are his victims. Martin de Kronung would have no reason to kill them."

"None that we know of," his wife added, "but if he had a reason I have no doubt he would kill anyone he wanted to." Changing the subject, she added, "I thought you were related to the king."
"My great-grandfather was a duke, but he had 18 children with two wives."
"That house must have been like Noah's ark at Easter."
Despite the difficult discussion with Martin de Kronung, the weather was still pleasant and the Hathaways refused to let him darken the day before the sun did – by going down.

Chapter 9: Immediate Dangers

The carriage to London left early the following morning. Along with the Hathaways and Mr BonHomme, there was a fourth passenger, a Lady Montparc. She spoke occasionally, complaining about everything and anything. The ride was too rough, the day too warm, the carriage too small. Nothing was right, but none of her complaints were aimed at the other three in the carriage, so on the whole the journey back to London was pleasant. Lady Montparc's presence, however, prevented the Hathaways from talking about what they had learned in their time in Canterbury and making some sense of it. If they had been alone in the carriage, they might have further discussed old Mary's information about Geoffrey or Linus. They might have discussed the Childes, especially as described by Martin de Kronung. They might have considered any number of points. As it was, they had to wait until they were back in London and back in their own home before discussing what they had learned.

*Übung 68: Übersetzen Sie die Sätze! Verwenden Sie dabei das Hilfsverb **might**!*

1. Sie könnten über die Childes sprechen.

____

2. Sie könnten über ihre Ergebnisse diskutieren.

____

3. Sie kämen schneller nach Hause, wenn sie die Kutsche nähmen.

____

4. Mr. de Kronung hätte freundlicher sein können!

____

5. Er könnte Recht haben.

____

“We only know”, said Mrs Hathaway, as she dressed for dinner that evening, “that Geoffrey de Kronung was part of the Childe family – even if he was distant from them. Linus? What connection could he have? And James de Bruyere and Mary FitzPaulding? I do not see any relation – they were de Bruyeres. That makes no sense. The Childes and de Bruyeres have no quarrel.”
“The de Kronungs and the de Bruyeres have no quarrel either,” Mr Hathaway said.
“Linus Groenig was allowed to grow up in the de Kronung household – why? Old Mary did not like his mother – did Susanne de Kronung?”
“We should have asked old Mary.”
“But old Mary said she was buried in a pauper’s grave”, Mrs Hathaway said, “and if Susanne de Kronung had liked her then she would have had a better grave.”

"True."

"It must have something to do with the father then."

"The father's name was Phip."

"Or perhaps," said Mrs Hathaway, a smile spreading across her face, "it was Philip. There is not much difference between Phip and Philip, you know."

"Philip who? There are thousands of Philips, my dear."

"Darling", Mrs Hathaway laughed, "there are thousands of Philips but only one Philip Childe – one of the children of Harold Childe who turned against their father."

"Just like Susanne. So Linus was the illegitimate son of Philip and therefore a direct descendant of Harold Childe like Geoffrey –"

"and Martin –"

"…de Kronung. But", said Mr Hathaway, "that explains only two of the four victims."

! ÜBUNG 69

*Übung 69: Lesen Sie weiter und fügen Sie die richtigen Hilfsverben ein! **(must (2x), be, can, need (2x), have to, shall)***

"You (1.) __________ to speak with Robert", Mrs Hathaway suggested, referring to Robert de Bruyere, "to find out something about his family background. There (2.) ___________ be some connection to the Childe family. There just has to be. You (3.) _________ to speak to him tonight."

"It (4.) _________ wait," Mr Hathaway decided.

"Tomorrow is Friday", Mrs Hathaway warned, "and a week from today someone else is going to (5.) __________ murdered. We have one week to find out who the murderer's next victim is and to try and prevent something horrible from happening."

"I absolutely have to go to work tomorrow," Mr Hathaway said. "Nevertheless I (6.) __________ visit him immediately after I leave the office," he added to calm his wife.

"Send a message to him that you will be coming, John. It is so important that you speak with him. He (7.) __________ not be at dinner somewhere else when you go there. You (8.) __________ warn him."

"I agree – but what can I warn him about? I have nothing specific."

"*He* might be in danger," said Mrs Hathaway.

"Robert can take care of himself."

"I am sure his cousin, James, thought he could, too."

"Anna, darling, you are getting too involved. Let us go down to dinner and not speak anymore on this topic," he said.

"But –," she began.

"– Shhhhh," he said, and taking the candle guided her down to the living room. Soon their guests would be arriving.

Just as he had promised his wife, Mr Hathaway was no sooner at work than he sent a man around with a message for Robert de Bruyere. The message asked for at least ten minutes of Mr de Bruyere's time. Mr de Bruyere wrote back that he had ten minutes for him, but that he and his wife were going to an important dinner and so he could not invite his friend to dinner. Mr Hathaway then sent a message to his wife, in order to calm her worries.

! ÜBUNG 70

Übung 70: Übersetzen Sie die Wendungen ins Deutsche!

1. make a suggestion

____

2. be the target of an attack

____

3. protect somebody from a danger

____

4. be the topic of a conversation

____

5. be involved in a quarrel

____

6. be the cause of her worries

____

Mrs Hathaway, however, was not a woman to stay at home when there was work to be done. Perhaps the FitzPaulding family had connections to the Childes. She decided to go visit the husband of Mary FitzPaulding and see what she could learn.

"This is a surprise," Simon FitzPaulding said as he entered the room where Mrs Hathaway was sitting. He was dressed in black and looked tired. Clearly the days were not getting easier as quickly as he would have liked.

Übung 71: Fügen Sie die richtigen Präpositionen ein!

ÜBUNG 71

"I am sorry to visit you (1.) ______ a time like this and to discuss a topic that will no doubt be unpleasant (2.) ______ you."

"What did you want to speak to me (3.) ______?"

Mrs Hathaway looked at Mr FitzPaulding. He was good-looking, with a strong chin. He and Mrs Hathaway had known each other more than ten years, but they had never had much contact (4.) __________ each other. She was uncertain of how to begin the discussion. She knew, though, that it had to be done, so she started.

"Four people have died (5.) _________ circumstances similar to those (6.) __________ your beloved wife. My husband and I are trying to determine why in order to stop the person responsible."

"Why you and your husband?"
"Why not?"
"The constables – what are they doing?"
"The one who has taken on the job is not moving quickly enough, my husband says."
"Well, what do you want from me?" He suddenly looked even more tired and depressed.

"I would like to know your family background."
"My family background? We come from nobility who once lived in the countryside and then two centuries ago moved to London. We have Saxon as well as Gallic background."
"Are there any Childes in your background?"
"No, I have no ancestors who were in the Childe family. Why?"
"We think that there may be a connection with the Childe family."
"I do not believe so. There are no members of that family in mine and none in Mary's."
"Are you sure?"
"Of course. You know how important these matters are."

ÜBUNG 72

Übung 72: Beantworten Sie die Fragen mit einer verneinenden Kurzantwort!

1. Do you want something from me?
   No, I don't.
2. Would he like to know my background?
   ______
3. Is she sure?
   ______
4. Have you talked to him yet?
   ______
5. Did he find the man?
   ______

6. Could you stay a bit longer?

____

7. Can you speak English?

____

"Her father was a de Bruyere, but her mother – do you know anything about her mother?"
"Her mother has no background."
"What do you mean her mother has no background?"
"I mean just that."
"But everyone has parents. Do you mean that she comes from another class."
"Precisely."
"Well, that is interesting."
"It is. Mr de Bruyere met her and fell in love with her and no matter what his parents said he would have no other partner than her. Rather than lose a son, altogether, they decided to welcome her into the family – though not with wide open arms. They bowed to necessity."

Übung 73: Fügen Sie die Wörter in Klammern in die entsprechenden Lücken ein!
(pattern, accepted, abandoned, potential, tally, clever)

Mrs Hathaway heard the explanation and (1.) ____________ it, but it was disappointing. It did not (2.) ____________ with the theory she had been developing. She was (3.) ____________ enough to know that if the theory did not work then it had to be

(4.) ____________ – but she also knew that it was the only theory she had.

"Thank you for your time," she said to Mr FitzPaulding. A servant saw her out to where her carriage was waiting.

As she was driven away, every face she saw on the street was a (5.) ____________ murderer while each carriage filled with nobility that she passed was transporting potential victims. There has to be a (6.) ____________, she said to herself.

Mr Hathaway met with Robert de Bruyere at an inn on Watling Street, as Mr de Bruyere had requested.
"I thought from your note," Mr de Bruyere explained, "that maybe the topic you wished to discuss would not be a pleasant one, so I suggested meeting here." He lifted a mug of mead, a sweet wine made from honey, and handed a second mug to Mr Hathaway.
"I am afraid it is *not* a pleasant topic. You know that Anna and I are trying to find out who killed your sister and cousin and two other young men."
Mr de Bruyere's face suddenly darkened. Several emotions – sadness and anger, especially – seemed to pass over it. "Why is Anna involved?" he asked at last.
"I could not stop her," Mr Hathaway answered, with a smile that showed he knew his counterpart might view him as weak.
"Your wife has a strong will," Mr de Bruyere admitted. "So what is it that you want from me?"
"Information, my friend." Mr Hathaway rested his hand on Mr de Bruyere's shoulder a moment. "I know about your father and his

family. The de Bruyeres are a well-known family. What can you tell me about your mother's family?"

Übung 74: Übersetzen Sie und enträtseln Sie das Lösungswort!

1. Honigwein _ _ ☐ _
2. Vorschlag _ _ _ _ _ _ _ _ _ ☐
3. Verbindung ☐ _ _ _ _ _ _ _ _ _
4. Streit _ _ _ _ _ ☐ _
5. Bitte _ _ _ _ _ ☐ _
6. Beschwerde _ _ _ _ _ _ _ _ ☐
7. Überlegung _ _ _ _ _ _ _ _ _ _ _ ☐ _
8. Beerdigung _ _ ☐ _ _ _
9. Angelegenheiten _ _ _ _ _ _ ☐

Lösung: _ _ _ _ _ _ _ _ _

"There is nothing to tell, as far as London society is concerned. I do not believe that she comes from a noble family."
"You do not *believe?*"
"Yes. That is the most I can say. My father made us promise never to discuss it. He never discussed it. The most he would ever say about their marriage is that he got married for love and not because his parents had arranged it. In fact, they certainly did not arrange it."
"In all the years that I've known you, Robert, I think I have seen your mother no more than ten times."

"That is just how she is. She likes to live in the background. She is a strong woman with strong opinions, but she does not offer them very often. Does this help you?"

ÜBUNG 75

Übung 75: Lesen Sie weiter und bilden Sie sinnvolle Wörter aus dem Buchstabenchaos!

"No," Mr Hathaway answered (1. lubntyl) ______________.

"What did you want to hear?"

"The (2. rutht) ______________."

"I have just told you the truth," Mr de Bruyere explained (3. yltenpati) ______________.

"I cannot believe that your father would marry someone outside of the (4. racystocira)______________. He was a man who believed strongly in tradition."

"He also believed in (5. dieobence) ______________," Mr de Bruyere said. "He told us not to ask questions about our mother's (6. dnuorgabkc) ______________ and so we did not – we have not."

"I believe that there is something that links all these murders together. It was no accident that your sister was chosen. All of the murders took place on Friday. The first three murders took place at two week intervals."

"So, you think that next week someone else is going to be murdered."
"One week from today. Unless the murderer is caught before, I am certain of it. The only other way to prevent the murder is to figure out who the next victim is. I do not think our chances are good."
"What do you think the connection is?"
"We believe that it has something to do with the Childe family."
"The Childe family? You mean Harold Childe and Leah Childe?"
"The very same. But given their status we cannot simply go to them and say this. Some thirty years ago, something happened in Canterbury which split the Childe family. The first two victims were on the side that rejected their father."

Übung 76: Formen Sie die Aussagesätze in Fragesätze um!

1. There is something that links the murders.

____

2. The murders have got something to do with the Childe family.

____

3. Next week, someone else is going to be murdered.

____

4. Someone from the Childe family murdered other family members.

____

5. Linus Groenig moved to London with Geoffrey de Kronung.

____

"Perhaps that is why they were killed?"

"Possibly – but thirty years later? That's a long time wait for vengeance and it would mean that someone in the Childe family murdered other family members. It is possible but I do not know if I believe it."

"James had a connection to the Childes."

"What was it."

"He was to be married to Leah Childe."

"I never heard that."

"Everything with the Childe family is secret," Mr de Bruyere explained. "They tell nothing. James told me only a week before he was murdered and he even told me that he was not supposed to tell anyone."

ÜBUNG 77

Übung 77: Setzen Sie die Sätze in die indirekte Rede!

1. "Everything with the Childe family is secret."

He said that everything with the Childe family was secret.

2. "James had a connection to the Childes."

____

3. "I never heard that."

____

4. "I do not believe that she comes from a noble family."

____

5. "He is to be married to Leah Childe."

____

6. "It seems to me that the Childe family has got a secret."

"Perhaps the Childe family know that they are in danger."
"Perhaps," Mr de Bruyere agreed. "Sorry, old friend, but I must be on my way. I am going to be late, as it is."
"Thank you for seeing me on such short notice," Mr Hathaway said.
"Anything for a friend. Besides, perhaps you will save my life."
Mr de Bruyere went through the door and into the darkness. Mr Hathaway stayed to finish his mead.

Chapter 10: Difficult Decisions

"There is nothing to be done," said Mrs Hathaway. "I will simply have to meet her and ask her questions directly."
"I do not think she will agree to see you," said her husband.
"Why not?"
"She is very private; she prefers to stand in the background."
"That may be, but she lost a daughter and now it is no longer the time to stand in the background."
"I have to work tomorrow morning," Mr Hathaway said, "so I cannot accompany you to Robert's house."
"Perfect. I am going to arrive unannounced. She is still living with Robert?"
Upon the death of her husband, Mrs de Bruyere had moved in with her son Robert and brought with her Robert's two younger brothers, Andrew and Harold.
"She is there permanently," her husband answered. "The boys are away at Oxford."

!

ÜBUNG 78

Übung 78: Lesen Sie weiter und setzen Sie die Verben in Klammern in die richtige Zeitform!

The following morning, immediately after breakfast, a time when she should not have been visiting anyone unannounced, Mrs Hathaway (1. stand) ________________ at Robert de Bruyere's door alone. She (2. be let in) ________________ and shortly after was greeted by Mr de Bruyere.

"What do you (3. want) ___________ with my mother?" he asked, when (4. tell) ___________ that speaking with her was the purpose of the visit.

"I have questions to ask her."

"For instance?"

"What is her name?"

"Clotilde."

"What (5. be) _________ it before she married?"

"That is something we do not talk about."

"I want to talk about it. It is important to talk about it."
"She is still upset about Mary's death."
"I know, but I want to stop future deaths."
"If my mother agrees to see you, I will sit with the two of you."
"I would prefer if you did not. Your mother might tell me something that she would not tell you."

"I do not believe so, Anna. Besides, I do not want her to tell you something that she would not tell me."

Übung 79: Übersetzen Sie, indem Sie den Infinitiv mit to verwenden!

1. Sie wollte darüber sprechen.

___

2. Mrs Hathaway erwartete, mit ihr sprechen zu können.

___

3. Sie wusste nicht, was sie tun sollte.

___

4. Sie wollte ihr viele Fragen stellen.

___

5. Sie zog es vor, persönlich mit ihr zu sprechen.

___

Mr de Bruyere led Mrs Hathaway to a rather dark sitting room and a moment later brought in his mother. The three sat together. The weather was threatening – at any moment a cold, September rain was going to begin to fall. In the shadows Mrs de Bruyere looked older and more hostile than Mrs Hathaway had expected. Mr de Bruyere, too, looked unfriendly. At first there was the usual small talk, but Mrs de Bruyere did not want to sit there all morning.

Despite what Mrs Hathaway had heard from Mr FitzPaulding and what her husband had learned from Mr de Bruyere, she could not look at the woman sitting across from her without feeling that she was a member of the aristocracy. She had a way of holding her head that showed pride and a sense of belonging.

! ÜBUNG 80

Übung 80: Unterstreichen Sie die richtige Variante!

"What did you wish to speak to me (1.) of/about?" she asked in a neutral voice.
"I am trying to find out who your (2.) daughters'/daughter's murderer is."
"That is no job for a lady of your status," she answered immediately.
"Perhaps not, but it is what I am doing just the same." Mrs Hathaway, too, tried to (3.) listen/sound neutral and yet serious, someone who could be forceful, if necessary. She had dressed (4.) in/with dark colours, not (5.) those/these of mourning but a grey that spoke of importance.
"We pay taxes", Mrs de Bruyere continued, "so that constables (6.) as well as/as soon as their assistants can maintain order."
"Yet they have failed to do so", Mrs Hathaway responded, "as you know better (7.) as/than I."

Mr de Bruyere looked at his mother, who stared back at him. They examined each other carefully. Mrs Hathaway thought that they were both going to stand up and ask her to leave immediately. She worried she might have forever ruined her husband's friendship with Mr de Bruyere.
"What do you want from me?" Mrs de Bruyere asked at last.

"There must be a connection between the people murdered. They were not chosen at random – or not completely at random. What can you tell me about your background?"

*Übung 81: Setzen Sie entweder **each other** oder **themselves** ein!*

ÜBUNG 81

1. Everybody is responsible for himself, so people must help ____________.
2. They are a family, so they should be there for ____________.
3. They met for the first time, so they didn't know ____________.
4. The Hathaways enjoyed ____________ on a warm and sunny day in Canterbury.
5. If they have no weapons, they can't defend ____________.

"I come from a modest background," the older woman answered immediately. "You might even say a low background. I have no name."
The two women stared at each other. It was something like a duel.
"I do not believe you," Mrs Hathaway said at last.
Mr de Bruyere was startled and made several noises but said nothing. Mrs de Bruyere stared straight back at Mrs Hathaway.
"What you believe will not change the facts," she responded. "It changes nothing."
"How many people have to die?"
"What?" asked Mr de Bruyere. "Really, this is too much."
"Look at your mother," Mrs Hathaway said. "Does she really look to you like someone who came from the lower classes?"
"I have never thought about it," Mr de Bruyere admitted. "She is my mother and that is enough."

ÜBUNG 82

Übung 82: Setzen Sie die richtigen Possessivpronomen ein!

"Look at her, then, and try to see her the way a stranger might. I have seen (1.) ______ mother twice in (2.) ______ life before today. I never once thought she came from the lower classes."

"Perhaps not," he agreed.

"But it does not change the facts," Mrs de Bruyere interrupted.

"(3.) ______ intuition", Mrs Hathaway continued, "tells me there is more to you than you admit. My intuition tells me that you hide because you have something to hide. My intuition says that you can tell me just what I need to know in order to come one step closer to stopping another murder taking place next Friday. (4.) ______ name is Clotilde. In Canterbury, I was told that one of the daughter's of Harold Childe was named Clotilde. Something happened thirty years ago and this Clotilde took sides against (5.) ______ father. Are you this same Clotilde Childe?"

"Naturally, she is not," Mr de Bruyere exclaimed and then there was silence.

"Yes, I am," Mrs de Bruyere whispered.

"You are?" her son asked. "Why did you keep it a secret for so long? The de Bruyeres have kept (6.) ______ distance from the Childes as long as I have known of them."

"And now you know why," she said gently, her voice now the voice of a mother.
"Actually, Mother, I do not know why."
"And that is my next question," Mrs Hathaway said. "What separated the Childe family so many years ago?"
"It is a secret," Mrs de Bruyere answered.
"That is an expensive secret," Mrs Hathaway responded. "It may have cost your daughter her life."
"That is too much," Mr de Bruyere shouted.

*Übung 83: **From** oder **of**? Setzen Sie die richtige Präposition ein!*

ÜBUNG 83

1. She came ______ a noble background.
2. They spoke ______ him with great respect.
3. She was the daughter ______ Clotilde de Bruyere.
4. She came ______ Canterbury.
5. She is a member ______ a convent.
6. Clotilde was ______ a noble descent.
7. She spoke with the voice ______ a stranger.

Mrs Hathaway sat there silently while Mr de Bruyere looked at her angrily. She looked from the son to the mother and back again.
"My husband said that he has learned that James was to be married to Leah Childe. It seems that the de Bruyere family was ready to move closer to the Childe family."
"We have been in contact," Mrs de Bruyere admitted. "About seven years ago, I started speaking to my mother and my brother again."

"Susanne died seven years ago."
"Susanne?" asked Mr de Bruyere."
"My sister. Susanne de Kronung."
"We are related to the de Kronungs? One of the victims was a de Kronung, right?"
"Geoffrey de Kronung," Mrs Hathaway confirmed.

ÜBUNG 84 !

Übung 84: Beantworten Sie die Fragen zum Text!

1. What was the plausible connection between the murder victims?

___

2. Why did Mrs Hathaway want to speak with Mrs de Bruyere?

___

3. What was Mrs de Bruyeres secret?

___

4. How were the de Bruyeres and the de Kronungs related?

___

5. Why was Mr de Bruyere so surprised?

___

"He was my cousin," Mr de Bruyere said thoughtfully. "How did you manage to keep all this from us?"
"Susanne wished to have nothing more to do with me, even after I rejected my father."
"You still have two de Kronung cousins, Martin and Arthur de Kronung," Mrs Hathaway said.

"Harold, my brother, heard from Martin and said he was a pompous, arrogant fool who did not know the first thing about honour."
"I met him", Mrs Hathaway informed them, "and I can tell you that if anyone is a murderer, it is him."
Mr de Bruyere sat in his chair speechless.

Übung 85: Lesen Sie weiter und ordnen Sie das Buchstabenchaos!

ÜBUNG 85 !

"So", Mrs Hathaway said, to get back to the questions she wanted to ask, "what (1. pislt) ________ the family apart? Did you fight over who would (2. hetirni) ________ the money or fight over how much each of you would inherit? Some of you were to get no money and so you disowned your parents because they were going to (3. sidwon) ________ you when they died, if not sooner?"
"I do not want to talk about it," Mrs de Bruyere answered.
"You have to," Mrs Hathaway said (4. ylndik) ________. "Everything may (5. pednde) ________ upon that. You had a sister named Susanne – and one of her children is dead. You had a brother named Philip and his (6. mateliletigi) ____________ son Linus Groenig is dead –"

"What?" Mr de Bruyere said.
"Your daughter is dead. I know you have a brother Claude, who is still alive, and a brother Bruce, who died. Do you have any other brothers or sisters besides Harold?"

"No."

"Did Claude or Bruce have children?"

"No."

"Then it is quite simple. The next targets will be the children of your brother Harold. Unless I am wrong and the murderer chooses your son," she nodded towards Mr de Bruyere, "or Martin or who knows?"

"Why are you doing this?" she asked. "It is not your family, after all."

"I am helping my husband", she answered, "who felt very strongly for your daughter and feels very strongly about your son."

"We rejected our father," Mrs de Bruyere cried out.

"You are his blood and so is Robert and so was Mary. You are guilty simply because of the blood which flows in your veins."

"I was eleven."

"That does not matter. Maybe you will be the next victim or maybe your brother will. Whoever it is, only you hold the key. Perhaps you can tell us nothing that will help us, but we are talking about family relations – your family. There are plenty more to die. Tell me, tell us, what happened."

! ÜBUNG 86

Übung 86: Welche Gegenteile gehören zusammen?

1. dead	☐ accept
2. simple	☐ innocent
3. wrong	☐ weak
4. strong	☐ alive
5. reject	☐ right
6. guilty	☐ difficult

"I cannot," Mrs de Bruyere said.
"Tell us, Mother", Mr de Bruyere said, "if it will save someone's life, if it will save Leah's life. She does not deserve to die any more than Mary did."
In answer, the older woman got up and slowly left the room, closing the door behind her without looking back.
Mr de Bruyere and Mrs Hathaway looked at each other, each a little surprised, each a little shy.
"Some secrets go to the grave," Mr de Bruyere said finally.
"Only if she is the next victim," Mrs Hathaway responded. "But that does not mean she will be the last one."

Chapter 11: Pieces of the Puzzle

Mr Hathaway left the office and decided to visit Constable Warwicke. Given the nature of their last meeting, he was not looking forward to seeing him again. He took a carriage to the constable's house and asked the driver to wait. A knock at the door brought at first no answer. Finally the door opened and the same woman he had seen the last time he had visited stared out at him.
"I would like to see Constable Warwicke please."
"He is not available," she answered and acted as if she were going to close the door.

Übung 87: Lesen Sie weiter und unterstreichen Sie die richtige Variante!

Mr Hathaway (1.) had pushed/pushed the door open, (2.) gently/gentle but (3.) forceful/forcefully, and ran up the stairs.

ÜBUNG 87 !

He turned to his left and knocked on the door.
"Really, you (4.) may not/shouldn't be here," the woman called from the bottom of the stairs.
There was no answer and so Mr Hathaway opened the door and walked in. He looked where he (5.) saw/had seen the constable's sword during the previous visit. It (6.) was gone/has gone.

"Where is he?" Mr Hathaway called.
"He's out."
The woman followed him upstairs.
He began looking around the rather large room. There was a bed and a desk and a few items hanging on the wall. Mr Hathaway looked at the objects hanging on the wall – a small tapestry, a portrait of two young men, an engraving of Canterbury and a coat of arms. Mr Hathaway went over to Warwicke's desk and got a piece of parchment, some ink and a quill pen. Quickly he sketched the coat of arms. When he was finished, he put everything back just as he had found it and walked to the woman waiting at the door to Warwicke's room, as if she did not dare enter.
"Where is he?"
"I don't know. He's been gone for five days now. I cook dinner for him every night, just in case he comes back and is hungry. He gets so angry these days if things are not exactly as he wants them. I've not seen him for five days."
"Do you know where he has gone or why? Did he tell you anything?"
"He never tells me anything."
"Who are the two boys in the picture?"
"Constable Warwicke and his brother."

Übung 88: Übersetzen Sie die Begriffe und enträtseln Sie das Lösungswort!

1. Kutsche □ _ _ _ _ _ _ _
2. Wappen _ □ _ _ _ _ _ _ _ _
3. Abendessen _ _ □ _ _ _
4. Gegenstände _ _ _ _ □
5. Skizze _ _ _ □ _ _
6. Gravur _ _ _ _ □ _ _ _ _
7. unteres Ende □ _ _ _ _ _
8. Federkiel _ _ _ □ _ _ _ _
9. Art _ _ _ _ _ □

Lösung: _ _ _ _ _ _ _ _ _

Mr Hathaway gave her a couple coins and she watched him go down the stairs and walk out into the street. Mr Hathaway got up onto the carriage and asked the driver to go to the de Bruyere house, where he was immediately allowed in.

“Well, your wife caused quite a stir here this morning,” Robert de Bruyere said, entering the room.

“Did she? I am truly sorry for that.”

“No need. I found out that I am a Childe on my mother’s side.”

Mr Hathaway showed his astonishment.

“I was quite certain that Anna was wrong,” he said. “I thought it was just a madman, but I thought it was better to make sure her theory was wrong. So, it was not.” He stood thoughtfully a moment. “Do we have any information on coats of arms here in London?” Mr Hathaway asked.

“The best place for that is where you just were – in Canterbury, at the cathedral there.”

Übung 89: Infinitiv oder Verlaufsform? Setzen Sie das Verb in Klammern in die richtige Form!

1. He began (look around) ______________ the room.
2. He went to the woman (wait) ______________ at the door.
3. She hated (be) ______________ yelled at by Mr Warwicke if something went wrong.
4. He wanted her (tell) ______________ him where the constable was.
5. She watched Mr Hathaway (go) ______________ down the stairs.
6. He knew it was important (find) ______________ the constable.
7. He could remember (ask) ______________ his wife, if she recognized anything.

"Send someone there," Mr Hathaway suggested. "I was just in Constable Warwicke's house, and he has a coat of arms."

"A constable with a coat of arms?"

"Exactly."

"What do you expect to learn? Where is the constable? You should ask him directly."

"He is gone at the moment. I do not know what I expect to learn. But when I saw the coat of arms, I remembered asking the constable – months ago – why the bodies of the people missing fingers were being taken to him."

"How did he answer?"

"He said that it was because he had asked the wagon driver to bring them by."

"In other words, he had taken on the responsibility."
"Yes, Robert."
"You think he might be our killer."
"I do", Mr Hathaway answered, "but I do not know why. Do you know where Anna was going?"
"Oh, yes, I do. I am afraid she was going to speak to Harold Childe and his wife." As Mr Hathaway stood to leave, Mr de Bruyere added, "I will send two of my people to Canterbury."
"They'll need this then," Mr Hathaway said, and handed over the drawing of the coat of arms.

Übung 90: Simple Present oder Present Progressive (Verlaufsform)? Setzen Sie die passende Form ein!

1. Harold Childe is speaking, and they (sit) ____________________ opposite Mrs Hathaway.
2. He (think) ____________________ that Warwicke is the killer.
3. What (Mr Hathaway do) ____________________ in Constable Warwicke's office?
4. At the moment, Anna Hathaway (speak) ____________________ with the Childes.
5. They usually (not travel) ____________________.

"I am afraid I cannot tell you anything," Harold Childe said.
He and his wife were sitting opposite Mrs Hathaway. The room was dark and candles flickered in several places around the room, splashing light here and there.

"I do not understand."
"We took oaths not to discuss what happened. I have not even told my wife."
"How did you find out?"
"We children were not supposed to find out, but we did."
"How?" Mrs Hathaway persisted.
"It is enough that we did find out."
"How did you manage to keep everything secret?"
"I did not manage anything. My father paid off many, many people. He paid them money and said he would kill anyone who revealed the secret. He even threatened to come back after he was dead. I remember that he said to my sister, Clotilde, that if she ever told anyone what she knew then he would stuff her tongue down her own throat until her face turned blue."
"He said that to his daughter?"
"He did. So, you can go home now. You understand that I am not going to tell you anything."
"And you, you understand that this might cost you your life or your sister her life? You understand your children are in danger as well?"

ÜBUNG 91

Übung 91: Finden Sie die deutsche Übersetzung für die englischen Wendungen!

1. take oaths

____

2. keep a secret

____

3. pay someone off

4. reveal a secret

5. stuff someone's tongue down their throat

6. cost someone's life

"We have servants and people paid to protect us. Nothing will happen to us."

"No one has ever seen the murderer in action. You have no idea who or what you are looking for," Mrs Hathaway challenged.

"The murderer", said Mrs Childe, "is flesh and blood, just as we are. He cannot go through walls."

"He may not need to." Mrs Hathaway got up to leave. Just as she was leaving their presence, she added, "I am not doing this to save your lives. I am worried about the de Bruyeres."

Mr Hathaway met his wife not far from their home. He paid his carriage and joined his wife in hers.

"How do things stand, my dear?"

"I spoke to Clotilde de Bruyere and to Harold Childe and neither are willing to tell me anything. They are both more afraid of dying at the hand of their father than the murderer."

"But their father is dead," Mr Hathaway said, unable to understand such a point of view. He shook his head. "I found a coat of arms at Constable Warwicke's house, and Robert sent off two men to Canterbury with a copy I made of it."

"What is he doing with a coat of arms?"
"Perhaps he is our murderer."
"Just because he has a coat of arms? John, that makes no sense."
"But it is suspicious. And that all the victims were brought to him first – why?"
"Why would a murderer have the bodies brought to him?"
Mr Hathaway had no answer, so he said nothing.

ÜBUNG 92

Übung 92: Setzen Sie die Wörter in Klammern in die Lücken ein!
(matches, reported, provided, exclaimed, woodstove, apparently, midday)

On Monday, at (1.) ____________, Robert de Bruyere visited Mr Hathaway in his office. The room was cool, despite a fire in a (2.) ____________ and several candles which (3.) ____________ light.
"My men came back late last night," he (4.) ____________. "There is a coat of arms which (5.) ____________ the one you drew. It belonged to a family named de Reuter. As you suggested, they asked for a Mr Smythe and he also found out that the de Reuters (6.) ____________ died out around 1282 or 1283. However, there was a Leonard de Reuter born in 1278 and a Roger de Reuter born in 1281."
"Leonard?" Mr Hathaway (7.) ________________, "that's the constable's first name."

Mr Hathaway left the office with Mr de Bruyere and returned once again to the constable's house and once again was greeted by the servant, who looked as if she cooked a lot but ate little.
"He's still away," she said.
"This makes no sense. Is he trying to find a criminal or just what is he doing?"
"He tells me nothing about his work. I know only what he likes to eat and when he prefers to eat. That's all I need to know and that's all I want to know."
While Mr Hathaway was wasting his time at the constable's house, Mrs Hathaway had made her way to the home of Mary Childe, wife of Harold Childe and mother of Harold, Clotilde and the others.
Laura Childe, who happened to be visiting her mother-in-law, confronted Mrs Hathaway in the sitting room. "What are you doing here? We have already given you all the information you have any hope of getting," she said arrogantly.
"I will let Mary Childe make the final decision on that," Mrs Hathaway responded.
"She is guided by her son in all decisions."
"Perhaps, but she will not refuse to see me."

Übung 93: Formen Sie die Passivsätze in Aktivsätze um!

1. She was greeted by the servant.

____

2. She was guided by her son in all her decisions.

____

3. She wasn't told anything about his work by him.

4. All the victims were brought to Constable Warwicke by the drivers.

5. The final decision was made by Mary Childe.

"There is nothing to be gained here."

"I will be the judge of that," Mrs Hathaway answered with finality.

A few moments later, Mrs Mary Childe was escorted into the room. She was an older woman, with a head of white hair hidden under a hat. Her dress was long and dark-coloured She looked tired, but it might have only been due to the weak light in the room. After greetings and polite small talk, Mrs Hathaway described the purpose of her visit. She provided the history – the murders which seemed to be somehow related and the reasons for the Hathaways' involvement, the death of Mary FitzPaulding. She described everything, leaving out only what it was she wanted from Mary Childe. When Mrs Hathaway stopped speaking, the older woman looked back at her with expectation on her face.

"What can *I* do for you?" Mrs Childe asked at last.

"In 1280", Mrs Hathaway began carefully, "something took place that permanently divided your family. I would like to know if it involved people outside your family and, if it did, just what happened. As I said, whoever is killing members of your family – and they are members of *your* family – is doing it for a reason. If you tell me what happened, possibly my husband and I can discover who is doing this and stop the murders. I promise you that your secret will not go beyond my husband and me."

Übung 94: Bilden Sie den Genitiv der Wörter in Klammern!

1. The (Childes) ______________ descendants.

2. The (constable) ______________ office.

3. (Mary FitzPaulding) ______________ death

4. She slept in one of the (servants) ______________ rooms.

5. He was married to his (boss) ______________ daughter.

6. She went to the (ladies) ______________ room.

7. She respected her (children) ______________ opinion.

"What you ask is not so easily done. I gave my word of honour to my husband, on his death bed, that I would not reveal what happened on that day."
"Not even to save his children?"
"His honour was worth more to him than the lives of his children," Mrs Childe said angrily. "A reputation is earned and lost."
"And bought, sometimes?"
"If necessary."
"If he did something that damaged his honour thirty-two years ago, then his honour has already been damaged, even if most of us are not aware of it. What is necessary now is that your children and your grandchildren no longer pay for the deeds of their father or grandfather. I do not see how you can put your dead husband's wishes above the needs of those alive today. He is already dead. You cannot bring him back. You can save your grandchildren."
The old woman looked at her and said, "I know what my duties are."

"You see", Laura Childe interrupted, "she does not wish to speak to you about this. You have no business being involved in this – you are not a member of this family and you are a woman."
"Laura, dear, please leave us," the elder Mrs Childe said.

ÜBUNG 95

Übung 95: Setzen Sie die Präpositionen ein!
(of (2x), after, over, for (2x), in)

When the door had closed (1.) ________ Laura Childe's departure, Mrs Childe said, "I tolerate no one speaking (2.) ________ me." Suddenly her voice seemed stronger, she seemed more decisive. "Thirty-two years ago, my husband took (3.) ________ the business of another man, a Mr de Reuter. This man claimed he had been cheated. My husband fought a duel with him. I was not there, but I heard they fought with swords (4.) ________ a very long time and (5.) ________ the end, my husband chopped off the right, little finger (6.) ________ his opponent. Normally, something like that should be impossible, but it happened. The wound itself was really minor, but he died (7.) ________ blood poisoning several months later. He had one boy and his wife was pregnant with another child when he died.

We gave them money for their silence. A few years later, his wife married another merchant, I do not remember his name anymore. He was a heavy drinker and drank away the money we gave them. I do not know anything more."

"Did your husband cheat the man?"
Mrs Childe stared at Mrs Hathaway with angry, green eyes. "My husband loaned him money which he could not pay back."
"He loaned him money at an unfair interest?"
"Most people", Mrs Childe responded, "today say that any interest is unfair. My husband took a risk and rightfully demanded payment for his loan. That is what my husband told me."
"And he paid many people in Canterbury to keep his secret, right?"
"Perhaps. I do not know."
"In any case, it seems clear that what he did was at least questionable."
Mrs Childe nodded in agreement.
"The duel took place on a Friday, I assume?"
Mrs Childe nodded again, unable to speak.
"And so", Mrs Hathaway continued, "it would seem that the children of the cheated man are now seeking to avenge the death of their father. Since they cannot say anything, they are avenging his death by killing your grandchildren."
"So it would seem," she managed to say.
"And you are content to let that happen?"
"Certainly not, but what can I do?" Mrs Childe said, the force coming back into her voice. "I first heard about it when Mary died."

Übung 96: Vervollständigen Sie die Sätze!
(questionable, avenger, cheating, interest, assume)

1. He got a loan from a moneylender at a high ____________.
2. What he said is ____________ because he is not a very honest person.

3. You don't trust a dubious person because he or she may be ________________.

4. Accepting something as being true without having a proof, means only to ______________ its truth.

5. If you take vengeance for an injury you are an ______________.

That night, Mr and Mrs Hathaway went to dinner with some friends. Afterwards, in the carriage on the way home, Mrs Hathaway said, "We have to find out where the boy and his brother or sister live."
"We know where one of them lives."
"Who is it?"
"It is, as I recently began to suspect, Constable Warwicke. After his father died, his mother married a merchant named Warwicke, who gave his name to both boys."
"The other one was a son, too?"
"Exactly. He was born just two months after his father's death."
"So, it has been Constable Warwicke all the time. Where is he?"
"Robert has sent out his men to search for Warwicke. If they find him, they are to stay with him and send for us."
"You be careful."
"We will. You can be sure."

There was a knocking and a banging at the door early Tuesday morning.
"Mr de Bruyere has sent for you," a servant said. "I have a carriage and can take you immediately."
"Bring in Johnson," Mr Hathaway said to his wife. "I want him to be with you at all times."
"I am in no danger," Mrs Hathaway said.

"If the constable finds out who is searching for him, he may come looking for me."
"You are not going to lock me up in a room, are you?" An ironic smile crossed her face.
"Not if I do not have to," he smiled back.
Mr Hathaway kissed his wife and left with the de Bruyere family servant.

Übung 97: Lesen Sie weiter und setzen Sie die Verben in die richtige Zeitform!

"Have you found him?" Mr Hathaway asked as he (1. be escorted) ________________ into the room where Mr de Bruyere (2. be seated) ________________.
"Possibly."
"We should leave immediately."
"We will – with a few of my men, as well."
Soon after a group of five men (3. leave) ____________ on horseback. They (4. ride) ____________ out to where there had been a report of Constable Warwicke. It was some 12 miles south-east of London, in the direction of Canterbury. After several hours, they (5. come) ____________ to a small village where they halted at an inn and rested the horses and (6. buy) ____________ something to eat for themselves. The men (7. drink) ____________ ale and ate a hearty meal.

"When we find our man", Mr de Bruyere said, referring to Constable Warwicke, "you leave him to me. He killed my sister Mary and I will have my vengeance."
After the meal and before they got on the horses, Mr Hathaway took Mr de Bruyere aside and spoke to him.
"Robert, you know it might not be Constable Warwicke," he warned.
"Why do you doubt that, after all we know?" de Bruyere asked.
"Firstly, it is hard to say just what the truth is at the moment. Secondly, Constable Warwicke has a brother and it could be his brother who has done all the murdering. We are not here to murder two men, are we, Robert?"
Mr de Bruyere looked away from Mr Hathaway and stared out into the open fields across which they would soon ride. "It was my sister," he said, forcefully.
"I know. I loved her, too. I just think we have to make sure that we do not murder an innocent person."
"Like you, I am here to stop a murderer, not to kill someone."
"Good," said Mr Hathaway, patting his friend on the shoulder.

! ÜBUNG 98

Übung 98: Finden Sie das „schwarze Schaf"!

1. refer to, ascribe to, appeal to, have to
2. retribution, distribution, punishment, vengeance
3. vigorous, forceful, impressive, depressive
4. guiltless, harmless, reckless, innocent
5. pat, strike, beat, kill

They mounted their horses and left the inn, crossing the fields. Some twenty minutes later, a small house, grey with the weather, came into view. Before they reached the house, however, a man walked out of it and stopped to watch them come up. Mr Hathaway recognized Constable Warwicke from a distance.

"What brings you here?" he called to the group of men when they stopped not far from him.

"We are here to stop the murders of the descendants of Harold Childe," Mr Hathaway said.

"Come in, gentlemen," Constable Warwicke said, and Mr de Bruyere and Mr Hathaway dismounted.

"If anything happens to us, if you hear anything", Mr de Bruyere said to his men, "come in immediately with your swords ready."

Mr Hathaway had his dagger out and his hand on the hilt of his sword.

"You will not need that," Constable Warwicke declared, but Mr Hathaway ignored him.

He led them into the house. The furniture was in complete disarray. It looked as if a storm had gone through the house. There was blood in a number of places.

"Who has been fighting?" Mr Hathaway asked.

"I have been."

"Who have you been fighting with?"

Constable Warwicke turned an ugly face at Mr Hathaway.

"My brother." He slowly removed his coat and showed an deep wound on his arm. "This one is worse than some of the others."

"You need to seek treatment," Mr Hathaway suggested.

"Treatment", he laughed, "is as likely to kill me as my injuries."

"Why have you been fighting your brother?" Mr de Bruyere asked.

Constable Warwicke turned an even uglier face upon him.

"That does not concern you."

"I am afraid it does", Mr de Bruyere responded, "because either you or he killed my sister and one of you is going to pay."

"Let me show you something," Constable Warwicke said, and led them over to a room. In front of it, on the floor, lay a thick, wooden door. "My mother had this door installed so that she could keep her money here, before my stepfather drank it away. For three months I kept my brother locked up in here."

"The three-month break before the murder of Mary FitzPaulding," said Mr Hathaway. He walked into the room, which had no windows and was lit by several candles. He saw blood on the floor and the mattress. "It must have been a fierce fight."

Mr de Bruyere followed Mr Hathaway in and agreed.

The door behind them closed. Not the one on the ground but one neither had noticed before. Both men began to yell but quickly realized that without windows and with thick walls on all sides their voices were not to be heard.

"Three men await him outside," said Mr de Bruyere confidently.

"I am afraid," a weak voice whispered, "that it will take thirty men, not three."

"Where did that voice come from?" Mr de Bruyere asked.

Mr Hathaway walked towards the mattress and looked around. They pushed the mattress aside and discovered a trap door in the floor. Mr Hathaway leaned over the door and looked at Mr de Bruyere who had his sword out. Mr Hathaway pulled back a piece of wood that had locked the door in place and raised the door. At the bottom of the hole beneath lay a man.

ÜBUNG 99

! *Übung 99: Wie heißt der Plural der folgenden Substantive?*

1. duty ______________________

2. headdress ______________________

3. thief ____________________

4. potato ____________________

5. church ____________________

6. baby ____________________

7. woman ____________________

8. horse ____________________

"Who is down there?" Mr Hathaway called.

Mr de Bruyere picked up a candle and used its light to illuminate the hole under the house.

"It looks like the fellow who just locked us in here," he said.

"The 'fellow' as you call him", explained the man, "is my brother. My twin brother."

Mr Hathaway took the candle and recognized Constable Warwicke – again.

"What are you – ?"

"I have a twin brother who is mad. It's the family secret: Every family has one, it seems, does it not?" he asked

"I will go down," said Mr Hathaway, his dagger still in his hand.

Mr Hathaway lowered himself into the hole. Mr de Bruyere handed a candle to him. Mr Hathaway examined the man by the light of the candle. The man's face and clothes were covered with blood. "It really is you", Mr Hathaway said, "and you are quite badly injured."

"My brothers did a good job. They worked together and did this. My twin brother has been helping my younger brother for two or three weeks now. My younger brother managed to escape from where I had him locked up and enlist the support of my twin brother."

"You should have brought him in to the court."

"And have my own brother executed?" he asked weakly. "Have a hand in the death of my brother? No, I couldn't do that."
Mr Hathaway helped Constable Warwicke to the opening. Together he and Mr de Bruyere managed to get the heavy man up.
"So, how do we get out of here, now?" Mr de Bruyere asked.
"I have no key," Constable Warwicke answered. "You have swords. You'll simply have to use them."
An hour or so later, the men managed to break through the door. Both were perspiring heavily and only succeeded because they were able to dismantle the door by using their swords. They immediately ran outside only to see that the three men who had accompanied them were laying motionless on the ground and two of the horses were gone.
"Was anyone else here?" Mr Hathaway asked.
"Aye", answered the constable affirmatively, "apparently my younger brother was here." He walked weakly. "I was in the room for nearly two weeks, I reckon, and they put me in the hole when I almost managed to escape two days ago."
"You have lost a lot of blood," Mr Hathaway observed.
"And I haven't eaten well," Warwicke added.
"Do you know where they might be going?" Mr de Bruyere asked.
"London," Constable Warwicke answered with an ironic smile.
"Why is your brother doing this?"
"I don't know who you are, but you should know that in the year 1280, my real father was cheated by Harold Childe out of his business. It was a swindle. My father, who believed in honour, according to my mother, wanted to deal with it legally but ended up dealing with it in a duel, where he lost his finger and eventually his life. My mother remarried but the man drank so much that the money the Childes gave us and any profits from his business went down his

throat. As a result, my brothers and I grew up in near poverty. I assume", he added, addressing Mr de Bruyere, "that you're a Childe."
"I just found out a few days ago."

Übung 100: Setzen Sie die Verben ins Simple Past und enträtseln Sie das Lösungswort!

1. wear _ _ ☐ _
2. fly _ _ ☐ _
3. drive _ _ _ ☐ _
4. hold _ ☐ _ _
5. mean _ _ _ ☐ _
6. begin _ _ ☐ _ _
7. throw _ _ _ ☐ _

Lösung: _ _ _ _ _ _ _

Once on horseback, Mr Hathaway asked the constable, "Are you and I to duel any time soon?"
"What're you talking about?" Warwicke responded.
"That tells me all I need to know."
During the ride back to the village, it became clear that Constable Warwicke could not ride the whole way. At the inn, they hired a carriage and went back together to London.
As they neared the city walls, it was already dark. Mr Hathaway asked, "Where did they go?"

"Do you know who their next target will be?" Mr de Bruyere asked.

"So many questions," Constable Warwicke exclaimed.

"You must have some idea," Mr de Bruyere insisted.

"There are many possibilities – either Clotilde or Harold; or, perhaps, young Harold or Leah Childe will be next, as none of the children of Harold have as yet been untouched. Susanne lost Geoffrey, Philip lost Linus, Clotilde lost Mary, and the others produced no children. Let's go to my house."

"They might be there," Mr Hathaway said.

"They might indeed."

A quick search of Constable Warwicke's house showed that they had gone elsewhere. Mr Hathaway and Mr de Bruyere left the constable at his house. They next rode to Mr de Bruyere's house and found that all was quiet there, too. They even accidentally woke Clotilde de Bruyere.

"I am going home," Mr Hathaway said. "We will have to put together some sort of plan, perhaps with Constable Warwicke, so we can stop the next murder. It's now Wednesday morning and in two days someone else is going to be murdered.

! ÜBUNG 101

Übung 101: Welches Wort ist das „schwarze Schaf"?

1. gain, win, acquire, accompany
2. unite, undo, join, connect
3. cowardice, bravery, courage, steadfastness
4. skinny, skilled, talented, trained
5. refuse, reject, decline, recall
6. doubt, uncertainty, disbelief, unwillingness

Mr Hathaway took a carriage home. As he entered his home, he noticed a small drop of blood near the door. Drawing his dagger, he quickly ran up the stairs, at the same time trying to remain calm. He took a candle into his bedroom and saw that his bed was empty. He looked around the room and came upon his wife, tied to a chair, some cloth stuffed into her mouth. She shook her head, but it was too late. A sword came down, knocking the dagger from Mr Hathaway's hand. He jumped onto the bed, and pulled out his sword, swinging it blindly until at length he hit a sword. Finally he could see his enemy. A moment later, a second person entered the room – Warwicke's twin brother.

"Back," Mr Hathaway ordered the twin.

The twin stepped back and waited a moment.

"Don't listen to him," came a sarcastic voice. "He's one of them, one of the ones who killed our father and made our life miserable."

"I saw him," the twin said.

"Out of my way," said the voice of the one with the sword.

It came too late, however. Mr Hathaway landed a blow on the arm. He could feel the bone through the sword.

"Out of my way, you idiot," the voice said, obviously in pain.

Mr Hathaway swung his sword again, as hard as he could and hit his opponent's sword. A rage took hold of him and he swung his sword again and again. He could no longer see his wife but the image of her sitting behind him, in a chair, tied up, shaking her head, inspired him to such a degree that he felt no fatigue. Again and again, he swung his sword but his opponent, even injured, was an excellent swordsman. He heard something fall behind him and turned around to see the twin leaping towards him. Mr Hathaway's sword swung in a complete circle and the blow landed on the head of the twin. He pulled his sword back and turned again towards the other brother who was now running down the stairs. Mr Hathaway ran after him, down the stairs, through the hall and pursued him out into the street. He saw the younger brother run down the street and then jump onto a carriage. There was a commotion in the carriage and it slowed. Mr Hathaway ran up to the carriage which had stopped in the middle of the street. There, on the floor, lay the younger brother, his life ebbing away, too weak from his wounds to get up.

! ÜBUNG 102

Übung 102: Ergänzen Sie das entsprechende Substantiv oder Verb!

1. complain ____________
2. ____________ prevention
3. discuss ____________
4. ____________ description
5. ____________ consideration
6. connect ____________
7. ____________ relation
8. ____________ quarrel
9. ____________ burial

"Call a constable," Mr Hathaway said. "Constable Warwicke. And send someone round to Mr de Bruyere."

A few minutes later many people were in the street. Mr de Bruyere came up to Mr Hathaway running.

"Please go to my house, Robert", he said, "and untie Anna."

Constable Warwicke was leaning over his brother and silently crying. "My baby brother," he said at last. "I couldn't stop him. I couldn't save him."

"What happened to you was unfair," Mr Hathaway said.

"I told him to stay in Canterbury and forget the past. Look at me, I started working my way back up. He was supposed to do that, too."

The dark street was lit by at least a dozen torches, and Constable Warwicke soon had both of his brothers laid out in a wagon. Mrs Hathaway was in Mr Hathaway's arms. Mr de Bruyere stood next to Constable Warwicke. "I am heartily sorry for your loss," he said. "Because you have suffered so, I shall not report your neglect of duty to your superiors."

"Thank you for that," mumbled Constable Warwicke and, with his head bowed, he trudged after the wagon, which was now bearing his brothers on their final journey.

"Well", sighed Mr de Bruyere, turning to the Hathaways, "we have achieved our objective and saved the life of the next victim, who-ever it might have been, and mainly thanks to the efforts of the two of you. You must be ready for a good night's sleep."

"Indeed we are," agreed Anna Hathaway, and all three walked away from the scene, leaving the crowd to gossip about what had actually taken place that night.

THE END

Abschlusstest

Übung 1: Ersetzen Sie ***might*** *durch die passende Form von* ***be allowed to*** *oder* ***it is possible that****!*

1. Might I come in for a minute?

____

2. They might not talk about the victims.

____

3. He might not be the right man.

____

4. The Childes and the de Kronungs might be two related families.

____

5. There might be a chance to get the information.

____

Übung 2: Ersetzen Sie in den folgenden Sätzen die of-Konstruktion durch den s-Genitiv!

1. The voice of the man sounded as if he were in pain.

____

2. They didn't know the next victim of the murderer.

____

3. He hit the sword of his opponent.

____

4. Mr Hathaway discovered the coat of arms of the constable.

____

5. It was the final decision of Mary Childe.

____

Übung 3: Bilden Sie sinnvolle Wörter aus dem Buchstabenchaos!

1. nizecogre ________________
2. dantnecsed ________________
3. gergad ________________
4. words ________________
5. sarraydi ________________

Übung 4: Setzen Sie die Verben in die richtige Zeitform!

1. Mr and Mrs Hathaway (know) ________________ each other for a long time.
2. He (talk) ________________ to Smythe at the moment.
3. He (meet) ________________ the constable before he spoke to his wife.
4. Last week they (go) ________________ to Canterbury.
5. They (live) ________________ in London for many years now.

Übung 5: Bilden Sie zu den folgenden Substantiven das passende Verb!

1. guide ______________________
2. approach ______________________
3. death ______________________
4. opposition ______________________
5. assumption ______________________

Übung 6: Formulieren Sie die Sätze im Passiv!

1. The constable didn't catch the murderer.

____

2. The murderer killed many people.

____

3. The carriage took them home.

____

4. They gave them directions to old Maria's house.

____

5. The Hathaways thanked Mrs Otsworth for her help.

____

Übung 7: Setzen Sie jeweils ***must/mustn't*** *oder* ***have to/don't have to*** *in die Lücke ein!*

1. You _______________ stay up late, if you are tired.

2. You _______________ lie to anybody!

3. They _______________ find out everything about the Childes.

4. A servant _______________ be loyal.

5. I _______________ do my exercises.

Übung 8: Welche Wörter haben eine ähnliche Bedeutung?

1. remain	☐ salesman
2. appropriate	☐ wealth
3. merchant	☐ determined
4. fortune	☐ stay
5. ambitious	☐ suitable

Übung 9: Setzen Sie die Sätze in die indirekte Rede!

1. "I have never met anybody like you!"

He said that he had never met anybody like him/her before.

2. "I don't want to join you."

____

3. "Wait for me in the carriage!"

____

4. “It seems that the constable is the murderer.”

5. “I saw him, when we were in Canterbury.”

Übung 10: Übersetzen Sie!

1. Mrs Hathaway wollte nicht in ein Zimmer eingesperrt werden.

2. Mr de Bruyere wollte, dass man ihm den Constable überließ.

3. Mr Hathaway sagte, dass Constable Warwickes Bruder der Mörder sein könnte.

4. Constable Warwicke stammte nicht von den Childes ab.

5. Constable Warwicke war verzweifelt über den Tod seiner beiden Brüder.

Lösungen

Übung 1: 1. People threw their waste onto the streets. 2. Most of the streets were small and narrow. 3. The man was holding the horse by the reins. 4. They kept moving through the streets. 5. A fresh wind was blowing from the countryside.
Übung 2: 1. What did he die of? 2. Where did he go to? 3. Who was he looking at? 4. What did he speak of? 5. What have you come for?
Übung 3: 1. The horse which pulled the wagon was old and tired. 2. The man is missing a finger. 3. Does the horse have a name? 4. He left the man as he was. 5. Is anything missing? 6. The constable was lucky that he didn't fall. 7. He should have left him where he found him.
Übung 4: 1. falsch 2. falsch 3. falsch 4. falsch 5. richtig 6. richtig 7. richtig 8. richtig 9. falsch
Übung 5: 1. better 2. earlier 3. more expensive 4. dirtier 5. gentler 6. more pleasant 7. richer 8. sadder 9. bigger 10. more
Übung 6: 1. looked 2. makes 3. was 4. said 5. is 6. have 7. makes
Übung 7: 1. different 2. uncomfortably 3. attentively 4. obviously 5. beautiful 6. cruelly
Übung 8: 1. in 2. on 3. of 4. at 5. at 6. from 7. of 8. in
Übung 9: 1. Being 2. recognizing 3. finding 4. think of 5. to leave
Übung 10: 1. was 2. involved 3. said 4. answered 5. asked 6. worked 7. was 8. was 9. could 10. heard
Übung 11: 1. Many different people frequented the inn. 2. Constable Warwicke sat in his accustomed corner every day. 3. It was difficult to provide the city of London with safe water. 4. This problem proved to be a challenge. 5. Mr Hathaway wanted to speak to Constable Warwicke.
Übung 12: 1. Am I allowed to ask the name of the victim? 2. They are not allowed to talk about the murdered man. 3. Are we allowed to come in? 4. It is possible that Robert de Bruyere and James de Bruyere are related. 5. It is possible that she is right.
Übung 13: 1. Mr Hathaway's wife was beautiful. 2. Mr BonHomme ignored the constable's words. 3. The last victim's name was de Bruyere. 4. Constable Warwicke's ale flew all over the table. 5. Mr Hathaway explained Warwicke's behaviour. 6. Constable de Luce was Warwicke's friend.
Übung 14: 1. himself 2. her 3. himself 4. herself 5. him 6. the...her 7. him 8. himself
Übung 15: 1. small 2. dark 3. half-lit 4. light 5. brown 6. deep 7. usual 8. deepest 9. great
Übung. 16: 1. action 2. light 3. loss 4. depth 5. femininity 6. holiness 7. danger 8. darkness Lösung: Clotilde

Übung 17: 1. heard 2. offer 3. answered 4. agreed 5. said 6. to speak 7. walked 8. finds 9. does

Übung 18: 1. It was Warwicke's duty to make the streets safe. 2. Mr BonHomme believed that Warwicke needed help. 3. For the constable it was a matter of honour to find the murderer himself. 4. Mr BonHomme criticized the constable's pride. 5. Many people moved to London which was becoming overcrowded.

Übung 19: 1. A good constable is able to find the murderer himself. 2. Wealthy people were able to make daytrips to the countryside. 3. There they were able to rest and relax. 4. She was able to ride a horse quite well. 5. Are you able to give us a tip? 6. Is anybody able to help us find the inn?

Übung 20: 1. kept 2. gone 3. Was 4. returned 5. spoke 6. were 7. seeing 8. unfolded 9. covering 10. missing 11. gaining

Übung 21: 1. met 2. stuffed 3. after 4. pale 5. become 6. ours

Übung 22: 1. upstairs 2. wooden 3. Constable 4. knocked 5. immediately 6. intensity

Übung 23: 1. at 2. on 3. in 4. from 5. in 6. In 7. of 8. of

Übung 24: 1. angrier, angriest 2. worse, worst 3. more friendly, most friendly 4. more difficult, most difficult 5. weaker, weakest 6. slower, slowest

Übung 25: 1. answered 2. loudly 3. allowed 4. responsible 5. could 6. offered 7. said 8. killed 9. murdered

Übung 26: 1. Where 2. What 3. Who 4. How 5. When 6. Whose/Which

Übung 27: 1. falsch (information) 2. falsch (progress) 3. richtig 4. falsch (people) 5. falsch (million) 6. richtig

Übung 28: 1. random 2. shaking 3. victim 4. pattern 5. perfectly 6. choice 7. excitement

Übung 29: 1. Is he from London or from Canterbury? 2. Were they in business with their murderer? 3. Have you got any information for me? 4. What standing are their friends? 5. Where were you when de Bruyere was murdered?

Übung 30: 1. administration 2. constable 3. body 4. carry 5. unbelievable 6. confused

Übung 31: 1. schlammig/muddy 2. unpassierbar/impassable 3. Diebe/thieves 4. Koffer/trunk 5. Dolche/daggers 6. gutaussehend/handsome 7. kahl/bald 8. Erscheinung/appearance 9. ärgerlich/annoying

Übung 32: 1. opposite 2. muddy 3. warm 4. young 5. creative 6. long 7. interesting

Übung 33: 1. responded 2. deliberately 3. absolutely 4. had 5. in 6. slept 7. for 8. information 9. which 10. something

Übung 34: 1. The Hathaways and Mr BonHomme travelled by carriage. 2. In Canterbury they hoped to get some information about Linus Groenig. 3. Mr Groenig was the first victim of the murderer. 4. James de Bruyere and Linus Groenig had both been stabbed. 5. Canterbury was about half the size of London.

Übung 35: 1. to experience 2. to guide 3. to approach 4. to die 5. to speak 6. to believe 7. to accompany

Übung 36: 1. by 2. to 3. in 4. from 5. of 6. on 7. from 8. for
Übung 37: 1. spectacle 2. pilgrim 3. baptism 4. prayer 5. record 6. chanting
Übung 38: 1. asked 2. entered 3. was 4. keep 5. were 6. pulled 7. come 8. ran 9. went 10. baptized
Übung 39: 1. be born out of wedlock 2. be listed in a record 3. be married to a man 4. go bright red 5. be baptized in a church
Übung 40: 1. He is an oblate at Canterbury Cathedral. 2. They are seeking information on Linus Groenig and Geoffrey de Kronung. 3. The father might have died before the child was born/Linus Groenig might have been born out of wedlock. 4. She turns bright red because the men are speaking of pregnant brides. 5. Because it isn't listed in the records of marriages.
Übung 41: 1. well-connected 2. proper 3. dark 4. brown 5. short 6. well-known 7. high 8. educated 9. comfortable 10. controversial 11. important
Übung 42: 1. They weren't sent to Canterbury by the constable. 2. Four people have been killed by the murderer. 3. The introductions were completed (by them). 4. They were introduced to Brother Ephraim by Smythe. 5. The circumstances were explained to Brother Ephraim by Mrs Hathaway.
Übung 43: 1. changes 2. is walking 3. are thanking 4. loves 5. looks 6. is observing
Übung 44: 1. fearfully 2. small 3. seriously 4. forcefully 5. unhappy 6. good
Übung 45: 1. falsch 2. richtig 3. richtig 4. falsch 5. falsch 6. richtig
Übung 46: 1. The building didn't have a straw roof. 2. He didn't think that London was a boring city. 3. Nobody was able to help them. 4. Mr BonHomme didn't want to be Mr Hathaway's second at the duel. 5. He wasn't murdered by a madman. 6. She didn't know anybody with the name 'de Kronung'.
Übung 47: 1. anything 2. of 3. for 4. ago 5. was 6. something 7. ever
Übung 48: 1. Do you know anything about the de Kronungs? 2. Does the family have connections with the merchant class? 3. Did she say anything about the background of Susanne de Kronung? 4. Would you like to stay for dinner? 5. What brought you to Canterbury? 6. Why do you want to find out who murdered him?
Übung 49: 1. answer 2. determined 3. wealth 4. salesman 5. stay 6. suitable 7. stack 8. aversion
Übung 50: 1. heard, heard 2. was, been 3. cut, cut 4. saw, seen 5. fought, fought 6. kept, kept 7. grew, grown 8. spoke, spoken
Übung 51: 1. London is the place to live. 2. Mr Hathaway was not the type to give up. 3. Was Mr Smythe a man to be trusted? 4. They were looking for a place to stay. 5. She wanted someone to care for. 6. Mr BonHomme was the only one to dislike Canterbury.
Übung 52: 1. ourselves 2. in 3. weather 4. then 5. have to 6. might 7. as
Übung 53: 1. don't have to 2. mustn't 3. must/have to 4. must/has to 5. don't have to
Übung 54: 1. knocking, got 2. following, got lost 3. hated, being 4. went, hesitating 5. climbing, saw

Übung 55: 1. healthy 2. waste 3. invitation 4. advice 5. walk 6. gentle 7. servant 8. inconvenience 9. charm 10. directions 11. yell 12. perfume Lösung: handkerchief
Übung 56: 1. c 2. c 3. b 4. b
Übung 57: 1. came 2. poured 3. appeared 4. died 5. remember 6. put 7. know 8. work
Übung 58: 1. richtig 2. falsch 3. richtig 4. falsch 5. richtig 6. richtig 7. richtig
Übung 59: 1. plague 2. employee 3. cheeky 4. pauper 5. protective
Übung 60: 1. her 2. she 3. they 4. her 5. you 6. I 7. he 8. their 9. you
Übung 61: 1. had just left 2. talked 3. gave 4. had stayed 5. visited
Übung 62: 1. since 2. for 3. since 4. since 5. for
Übung 63: 1. thorough 2. silence 3. unpleasant 4. while 5. realized 6. being 7. anger 8. mourning
Übung 64: 1. While speaking of Linus Groenig, Mr de Kronung couldn't hide his anger. 2. Mr de Kronung thought his brother was murdered because he went into business. 3. Linus Groenig ran a successful business in London. 4. Martin de Kronung didn't seem to be very grief-stricken. 5. If Groenig hadn't been murdered, he might have killed him himself.
Übung 65: 1. yet 2. if 3. have 4. about 5. younger 6. more reckless 7. thought 8. happened
Übung 66: 1. falsch 2. richtig 3. richtig 4. richtig 5. falsch 6. richtig 7. falsch 8. falsch
Übung 67: 1. Then they fell asleep. 2. I think he is a true nobleman. 3. He is very respectable. 4. He likes being a merchant. 5. They are his victims.
Übung 68: 1. They might talk about the Childes. 2. They might discuss their results. 3. They might get home quicker, if they took the carriage. 4. Mr de Kronung might have been more friendly. 5. He might be right.
Übung 69: 1. need 2. must 3. need 4. can 5. be 6. shall 7. must 8. have to
Übung 70: 1. einen Vorschlag machen 2. das Ziel eines Angriffs sein 3. jemanden vor einer Gefahr bewahren 4. Gegenstand einer Unterhaltung sein 5. in einen Streit verwickelt sein 6. der Grund für ihre Sorgen sein
Übung 71: 1. at 2. for 3. about 4. with 5. under 6. of
Übung 72: 1. No, I don't. 2. No, he wouldn't. 3. No, she isn't. 4. No, I haven't. 5. No, he didn't. 6. No, I can't. 7. No, I can't.
Übung 73: 1. accepted 2. tally 3. clever 4. abandoned 5. potential 6. pattern
Übung 74: 1. mead 2. suggestion 3. connection 4. quarrel 5. request 6. complaint 7. consideration 8. burial 9. matters Lösung: ancestors
Übung 75: 1. bluntly 2. truth 3. patiently 4. aristocracy 5. obedience 6. background
Übung 76: 1. Is there something that links the murders? 2. Have the murders got something to do with the Childe family? 3. Is someone else going to be murdered next week? 4. Did someone from the Childe family murder other family members? 5. Did Linus Groenig move to London with Geoffrey de Kronung?

Übung 77: 1. He said that everything with the Childe family was secret. 2. He said that James had had a connection to the Childes. 3. He said that he had never heard that. 4. He said that he didn't believe that she came from a noble family. 5. He said that he was to be married to Leah Childe. 6. He said that it seemed to him that the Childe family had got a secret.
Übung 78: 1. was standing/stood 2. was let in 3. want 4. told 5. was
Übung 79: 1. She wanted to talk about it. 2. Mrs Hathaway expected to speak with her. 3. She didn't know what to do. 4. She wanted to ask her many questions. 5. She preferred to speak with her personally.
Übung 80: 1. about 2. daughter's 3. sound 4. in 5. those 6. as well as 7. than
Übung 81: 1. themselves 2. each other 3. each other 4. themselves 5. themselves
Übung 82: 1. your 2. her/my 3. My 4. Your 5. her 6. their
Übung 83: 1. from 2. of 3. of 4. from 5. of 6. of 7. of
Übung 84: 1. They had a connection to the Childe family. 2. She wanted to find out something about the Childe family. 3. She was Clotilde Childe. 4. Mrs de Bruyere was Susanne de Kronung's sister. 5. He was surprised because he didn't know anything about his family's secrets.
Übung 85: 1. split 2. inherit 3. disown 4. kindly 5. depend 6. illegitimate
Übung 86: 1. alive 2. difficult 3. right 4. weak 5. accept 6. innocent
Übung 87: 1. pushed 2. gently 3. forcefully 4. shouldn't 5. had seen 6. was gone
Übung 88: 1. carriage 2. coat of arms 3. dinner 4. items 5. sketch 6. engraving 7. bottom 8. quill pen 9. nature Lösung: constable
Übung 89: 1. looking around 2. waiting 3. being 4. to tell 5. going 6. to find 7. asking
Übung 90: 1. are sitting 2. thinks 3. is Mr Hathaway doing 4. is speaking 5. don't travel
Übung 91: 1. einen Eid leisten 2. ein Geheimnis bewahren 3. jemanden ausbezahlen 4. ein Geheimnis aufdecken 5. jemandem das Maul stopfen *fam* 6. jemanden das Leben kosten
Übung 92: 1. midday 2. woodstove 3. provided 4. reported 5. matches 6. apparently 7. exclaimed
Übung 93: 1. The servant greeted her. 2. Her son guided her in all her decisions. 3. He didn't tell her anything about his work. 4. The drivers brought all the victims to Constable Warwicke. 5. Mary Childe made the final decision.
Übung 94: 1. Childes' 2. constable's 3. Mary FitzPaulding's 4. servants' 5. boss's 6. ladies' 7. children's
Übung 95: 1. after 2. for 3. over 4. for 5. in 6. of 7. of
Übung 96: 1. interest 2. questionable 3. cheating 4. assume 5. avenger
Übung 97: 1. was escorted 2. was seated 3. left 4. were riding 5. came 6. bought 7. drank

Übung 98: 1. have to 2. distribution 3. depressive 4. reckless 5. kill
Übung 99: 1. duties 2. headdresses 3. thieves 4. potatoes 5. churches 6. babies 7. women 8. horses
Übung 100: 1. wore 2. flew 3. drove 4. held 5. meant 6. began 7. threw Lösung: revenge
Übung 101: 1. accompany 2. undo 3. cowardice 4. skinny 5. recall 6. unwillingness
Übung 102: 1. complaint 2. prevent 3. discussion 4. describe 5. consider 6. connection 7. relate 8. quarrel 9. bury

Lösungen Abschlusstest

Übung 1: 1. Am I allowed to come in for a minute? 2. They are not allowed to talk about the victims. 3. It is possible that he is not the right man. 4. It is possible that the Childes and the de Kronungs are related. 5. It is possible to get the information.
Übung 2: 1.The man's voice sounded as if he were in pain. 2. They didn't know the murderer's next victim. 3. He hit his opponent's sword. 4. Mr Hathaway discovered the constable's coat of arms. 5. It was Mary Childe's final decision.
Übung 3: 1. recognize 2. descendant 3. dagger 4. sword 5. disarray
Übung 4: 1. have known 2. is talking 3. met 4. went 5. have lived
Übung 5: 1. to guide 2. to approach 3. to die 4. to oppose 5. to assume
Übung 6: 1. The murderer wasn't caught by the constable. 2. Many people were killed by the murderer. 3. They were taken home in the carriage. 4. They were given directions to old Maria's house. 5. Mrs Otsworth was thanked for her help (by the Hathaways).
Übung 7: 1. don't have to/mustn't 2. mustn't 3. must/have to 4. must 5. have to/must
Übung 8: 1. stay 2. suitable 3. salesman 4. wealth 5. determined
Übung 9: 1. He said that he had never met anybody like him/her before. 2. He said that he didn't want to join him/her. 3. He said that he should wait for him/her in the carriage. 4. He said that it seemed that the constable was the murderer. 5. He said that he had seen him when they were/had been in Canterbury.
Übung 10: 1. Mrs Hathaway didn't want to be locked up in a room. 2. Mr de Bruyere wanted the constable to be left to him. 3. Mr Hathaway said that Constable Warwicke's brother could be the murderer. 4. Constable Warwicke was not a descendant of the Childes. 5. Constable Warwicke was distraught about the death of his two brothers.